Clear Speech

Pronunciation and
Listening Comprehension
in North American English

Second Edition

Teacher's Resource Book

Judy B. Gilbert

CAMBRIDGE
UNIVERSITY PRESS

Published by the Press Syndicate of the University of Cambridge
The Pitt Building, Trumpington Street, Cambridge CB2 1RP
40 West 20th Street, New York, NY 10011-4211, USA
10 Stamford Road, Oakleigh, Melbourne 3166, Australia

© Cambridge University Press 1984, 1993

First published 1984
Second edition 1993

Printed in the United States of America

ISBN 0-521-42116-0 (Teacher's Resource Book)
ISBN 0-521-42118-7 (Student's Book)
ISBN 0-521-42117-9 (Cassette Set)

Design, layouts, and text composition: Adventure House, Inc.

Cassette production by The Sun Group. The recording of Louis Moreau Gottschalk's "Pasquinade,"
played by Eugene List, courtesy of Omega Record Group, Inc., New York, New York.

Contents

Contents

Preface

Here is a sad story: The teacher has just completed a successful pronunciation lesson using minimal pairs of words to teach the sounds **R** and **L**. All of the students have been able to manage the distinction by the end of the lesson. The students feel good and the teacher feels good. Then, as the students are leaving the room, one turns to the teacher and says cheerily, "So rong!" The teacher does not feel so good any more.

The fact is, minimal pair practice alone sometimes seems to yield minimal results. This may be part of the reason the teaching of pronunciation has fallen into disfavor in so many programs. Lack of success is discouraging to teachers, and students sometimes feel that pronunciation is an endless succession of unrelated and unmanageable pieces. If the work is so discouraging, shouldn't we just drop it? Why should we include pronunciation in the curriculum?

There are two fundamental reasons to teach pronunciation:

1. Speech clarity (the ability to be understood easily)
2. Listening comprehension (the ability to follow spoken language)

Without both of these abilities, attempts at conversation with an English speaker are apt to break down in embarrassment or even annoyance. Repeated breakdowns are discouraging, and this tends to cut the learner off from further opportunities to improve.

Pronunciation and listening comprehension are linked together. Furthermore, they are linked by a unified system within which the individual sounds are systematically related. Students need this sense of system in order to make sense of the separate pieces. A specific example of a pronunciation topic which affects listening comprehension is the common use of contractions in the spoken language. Contractions are not used simply to speed up communication, but as part of the sytem of basic emphasis. When students understand this, they can listen more effectively.

Conscientious teachers ask, "How can we reduce student errors?" It may be more useful to turn that question around this way: "How can we increase student clarity?" *Clear Speech* is designed to help achieve this goal.

Linguistic framework

This textbook is based on the principle that rhythm and melody (and their effect on sentence emphasis and thought grouping) are the framework within which speech flows most clearly from speaker to listener.

Use of the Teacher's Resource Book

Every unit begins with general comments on the topic and then proceeds with specific suggestions and answers for the exercises. The first unit, "Rhythm: number of syllables," makes specific suggestions for the various types of exercises used throughout the Student's Book. Therefore, even if you do not plan to teach Unit 1, you may find it useful to read that section for general teaching tools.

Acknowledgments

I would like to thank the more than seventy teachers from the following institutions who have given time and attention to field-testing the successive drafts of this new edition. Their efforts have been important in making this book easier to teach.

American Language Institute, Mariánské Lázně, Czech Republic
Andrews University, Michigan, USA
Camosun College, British Columbia, Canada
Contra Costa College, California, USA
English Language Center, California, USA
ELS Language Center, Ohio, USA
Essex County College, New Jersey, USA
George Mason University, Virginia, USA
Georgia Institute of Technology, Georgia, USA
Georgia State University, Georgia, USA
Harvard University, Massachusetts, USA
Hokuriku University, Kanazawa, Japan
Iowa State University, Iowa, USA
Johns Hopkins University, Maryland, USA
Marymount College, New York, USA
Mohawk College, Ontario, Canada
New Brunswick Community College, New Brunswick, Canada
New York University, New York, USA
Nova University, Florida, USA
Oregon State University, Oregon, USA
Sacramento City College, California, USA
Santa Clara Adult Education, California, USA
São Paulo Catholic University, São Paulo, Brazil
SGI-Workplace ESL, California, USA
Sheridan College, Mississauga, Canada
Stanford University, California, USA
University of Georgia, Georgia, USA
University of Maryland, Maryland, USA
University of Michigan, Michigan, USA
University of Tennessee, Martin, Tennessee, USA
Vanderbilt University, Tennessee, USA
Vysoká Škola Strojní a Textilní, Liberec, Czech Republic
Xavier University, Ohio, USA
York University English Language Institute, Ontario, Canada

Introduction

New edition

The second edition of *Clear Speech* was written because teachers who were using the first edition asked for more practice material. In the course of three years of field testing, it became apparent that the text could be made more teachable by re-arranging and "spiraling" the basic concepts. It also became apparent that students wanted individual sounds addressed first. The difficulty with putting these smaller units of language first is that classes have a tendency to bog down in the effort to perfect the sounds and, therefore, don't have enough time to go on to more useful work on rhythm, intonation, and thought grouping. To solve this difficulty, the course now presents sounds in a way that requires the students to think about how certain qualities of sounds affect meaning. This approach not only makes possible an early and systematic introduction to rhythm and linking during the practice of sounds, but also encourages students to think about sounds in a larger context.

Field testing

The explanations and comments in this Teacher's Resource Book were developed as a result of field testing by more than seventy teachers, all of whom had different backgrounds and teaching situations. Many of the practical suggestions came directly from the field-test teachers. Some of the problems discussed may never occur in your class, just as some of the material in the text will fit your particular situation better than will other parts of the book.

Main aspects of the Student's Book

The text begins with optional listening and speaking tests. Then each teaching point is presented through a variety of exercises. The main approach is Pair Practice activities, but there are also mouth illustrations, dictations, poems, games, Check Yourself exercises (self-monitoring activities), and listening tasks. There are also quizzes and short lectures in the Teacher's Resource Book.

Clear Listening Test, Clear Speaking Test

The Clear Listening Test takes about 20 minutes and is useful as a pre- and post-course test. It can be given to large numbers of students, either using the cassette or being read aloud by the teacher. The Clear Listening Test makes the student aware of which aspects of pronunciation need improvement; it also provides the teacher with a general picture of the class. Because improved scores on the post-course test depend upon the students' having been adequately exposed to the main concepts tested, it is better not to give a posttest if there has not been time to teach all the concepts.

The Clear Speaking Test must be recorded by the student and then analyzed. The test is in the form of a dialogue to test students' understanding of shifting focus, connections between sentences, and different types of final intonational contours. To simplify the teacher's review of the recording, an analysis form that lists some common errors is provided on page 63 in this Teacher's Resource Book. Additional errors can be noted on the analysis form. A post-course recording can demonstrate some of the progress the student has made.

Pair practice

Each unit contains several exercises requiring students to work in pairs. This allows each student time for essential speaking practice and also provides immediate feedback on errors. Both students are actively involved throughout the exercise since the listening is as important as the speaking.

Pair practice activities decrease the amount of tension a student may feel because the activity is relatively private. Tension is counterproductive in any language-learning situation, but this is especially true in a pronunciation class. Even if the teacher is circulating around the room and giving individual attention to the student pairs, the effect is more relaxed than when a student is reciting in front of the entire class.

Another advantage of pair activities is that the game-playing aspect of this approach keeps everybody alert and involved. For variety, the teacher can use these exercises for listening practice or for quizzes, with the teacher playing the role of Student 1. More specific suggestions for managing pair practice activities are given in Units 1 and 2.

Mouth illustrations

Entirely new illustrations of the vocal tract are provided in the second edition to aid students in understanding how sounds are made. The teeth are shown in relation to the tongue, and views are given from above in order to aid students' perception of air flow distinctions between different types of sounds. Specific advice on helping students to understand these drawings is given in Unit 2.

Linking

In the first edition of *Clear Speech,* linking was presented in a separate lesson. However, linking was found to be such an important phenomenon that it is recycled frequently throughout the early lessons in this new edition. Recycling the concept increases students' command of linking and is also useful for focusing attention on important sound differences at the end of words. Specific suggestions for presenting linking are given in Unit 2.

Dictation

Dictations can be given by using the cassettes or by reading aloud from the answers for that particular unit. Procedures are discussed in Unit 1.

Check Yourself

Self-monitoring is a necessary part of long-range improvement. Check Yourself exercises are best done with a tape recorder if at all possible. Students generally find recording useful, as soon as they get over their uneasiness about hearing their own recorded voices.

Review

Each unit ends with one or more review exercises. These reviews recycle concepts taught earlier in order to further solidify students' mastery of concepts. All teaching points are tied together in a spiral fashion throughout the book, partly by means of the reviews and partly by expanding on the relationships between the points.

Use of the cassettes

The cassette symbol (▭) indicates material in the Student's Book and the Teacher's Resource Book that is recorded on the two accompanying cassettes. Play the cassettes or read the text aloud for listed exercises. Pause after the first time a sentence is dictated or during involved listening tasks so that students have time to write or make marks in between the repetition of the same item. That way they can check their work when they hear it the second time. The class may need to hear listening material more times than provided on the cassette. Students can also use the cassettes for self-study and in the language laboratory.

Contractions and reductions

Language learners often complain that native speakers "talk too fast" and that they get headaches from trying to listen to the news on English-language radio programs or when attempting to carry on a conversation in English. Two aspects of English pronunciation increase this sense that the language is too fast: linking of words and reductions. If an English learner cannot sort out the meaning of the question "Izzybusy?" (Is he busy?), an appropriate response will be impossible. Because contractions and reductions are a major problem in listening comprehension, *Clear Speech* puts a lot of emphasis on teaching these aspects of pronunciation. Some psychological ramifications of this topic are discussed in Unit 4.

Limericks

Short bits of light poetry are used for a different kind of practice of the rhythm point in a specific lesson. Highly rhythmic material helps students "swing" into the rhythm patterns being taught and also provides a change of pace. Specific suggestions for using the poetry are given in Unit 2.

Vocabulary

Clear Speech is intended for a wide variety of teaching situations, so it is inevitable that some vocabulary will not be familiar to your students. Specific discussion of this issue is presented in Unit 1.

Homework

If your students are in an English-speaking environment (or have access to English broadcasts), it is productive to ask them to listen for one or two examples of the pronunciation point you are teaching. This could range from listening for a word that ends in a stop, a word with four syllables, or a contraction, to the more advanced task of listening for emphasis on a focus word. Asking for just one or two examples is apt to focus students' attention better than asking for many examples because it is exceptionally difficult for people to listen for a pronunciation point at any length when they are also trying to follow the meaning of spoken language. If they actually identify an example, they will have concentrated enough to demonstrate true understanding of the teaching point.

If you have time to go over student recordings, ask students to make regular tapes of some of the dialogues or limericks, plus a little free conversation. Point out a few errors on each, especially those that relate to the current lesson topic. Students appreciate this personal attention.

Preparation for the TOEFL

Many students are so worried about preparing for the TOEFL that they are reluctant to spend class time on pronunciation; they do not see how it will help their score on the examination. Although it is true that the TOEFL does not test directly for pronunciation, you can assure students that work in this course can help them in both the listening and reading comprehension parts of the TOEFL. Work on listening for contractions, reductions, and word linking enhances listening comprehension. In the same way, work on intonation can improve reading skills. This is because learning to recognize the "road signs" of language, in order to get oriented and to predict what may be coming next, is fundamental to rapid language comprehension, spoken or written.

Answers to the exercises

Answers are provided for checking exercises and for giving dictations. The answers are based on general usage, but dialect variations may cause differences from your own experience.

Quizzes

Quizzes are provided to be used at eight points in the course. There are two purposes for the quizzes: (1) If students miss a few answers, they can see the need for further practice, and (2) the quizzes give the teacher a profile of the students' listening weaknesses, which, in turn, is likely to be a good profile of pronunciation weaknesses. The quizzes can be photocopied and distributed in class as required. The answers to the quizzes can be found on pages 67–69 in this Teacher's Resource Book.

Lectures

Lectures on topics relevant to pronunciation learning and public speaking are included for listening comprehension practice, beginning on page 48.

Glossary

Terms used in the Student Book are explained in nontechnical language suitable for student comprehension. The glossary begins on page 70.

Priorities

If the time allowed for this course is short, it is recommended that you teach Units 1, 8, 9 (rhythm) and Units 11–14 (emphasis) first to ensure that students have time to consolidate understanding of these most important topics.

Within the units on sounds (Units 3–7), give a high priority to linking exercises.

Index to sounds

1 Rhythm: number of syllables

This course begins with a discussion of syllable number because syllables are an essential foundation for English rhythm. Rhythm may be the single most important element in learning clear pronunciation. There may also be consequences for learning grammar. Teachers sometimes notice that students with an instinct for the rhythm of English seem to have better control of the structure words (for instance, articles) that are often missing from other students' speech. This may be at least one reason why teenage English learners who spend a lot of time listening to popular music in English sometimes seem to "catch on" to grammar rules more quickly than others.

An awareness of syllables is important because it helps students:

1. Identify the exact syllable for stress marking, which the native speaker relies on for clear understanding (e.g., the difference between "desert" and "dessert")
2. Notice reduced syllables, such as articles, auxiliaries, and word endings, often missing from students' speech (e.g., "Where post office?" and "I rent the car yesterday.")
3. Become sensitive to English rhythm ("this is" and "this" are rhythmically different)

Following are some cross-language comparisons of syllable number that you can put on the board. The information in the charts provides an enlightening exercise for some students.

These comparison words are meant as rough examples. Your students may spell these words differently or even pronounce them differently because of dialect variations (which is also true of English), but the comparisons can be quite helpful.

Spanish	English
↓↓↓↓ chocolate	↓ ↓ chocolate
↓↓ clase	↓ class
↓↓↓↓ telefono	↓↓ ↓ telephone

Japanese	English
↓↓↓↓ chokoletto	↓ ↓ chocolate
↓↓↓ kokoa	↓↓ cocoa
↓↓↓ terebi	↓↓ TV
↓↓↓ miraku	↓ milk

Arabic	English
↓ ↓ lamba	↓ lamp
↓ ↓ kimie	↓↓↓ chemistry

French	English
↓ ↓ français	↓ French
↓↓↓ assurer	↓↓ assure

German	English
↓↓↓↓ Schokolade	↓ ↓ chocolate
↓↓ kakao	↓↓ cocoa

Russian	English
↓↓ banan	↓↓↓ banana
↓↓ vasa	↓ vase

"Chocolate" is such a common "loan" word that many students may be able to supply a version from their languages. You can also ask for the words for "tea," "sugar", "chess," or other shared words that might occur to you or your students.

Unfamiliar vocabulary

Because students like to know what they are saying, they are likely to be more satisfied with the exercise if you can define a new word quickly. However, it is not good to allow too much valuable class time to be absorbed by discussion of vocabulary. For that reason, it can help to assign unknown words as dictionary work before the class. If vocabulary you haven't assigned turns out to be a problem, assign it as homework for *after* the class. The advantage of this type of homework is that it will then provide an automatic occasion for review of the teaching point when students bring the words back to class. The main object should always be to keep students' attention focused on pronunciation and its effect on meaning.

Dictionaries give not only meanings but also syllabification. To prepare for this type of homework, you can show the students how syllables are marked in their dictionaries. If your students are using different dictionaries, a good homework task is to study how to tap out the markings in each dictionary. The different systems of marking syllables could be discussed in class if time is available. In any case, the students need to learn how to use their dictionaries as a resource in the syllabification and stress of words.

A

Counting syllables 🔲

Play the cassette or read aloud the lists of words first across, then in random order. Have students tap their hands on their desks to count the syllables. Then call on individuals to tell how many syllables are in a given word. Another possibility is to have the class hold up the number of fingers for the number of syllables in each word. In this method, it is possible to check the entire class at a glance.

There are specific problems for Japanese students counting syllables: Japanese de-voices the high vowels (as in the English words "eat" and "boot") between voiceless consonants or between a voiceless consonant and silence (as at the end of a word). Therefore, "sukiyaki" is apt to sound like it has three syllables to the English listener, and "Hiroshi" is apt to sound like it has two syllables.

Another problem for Japanese students is that they count nasals (**N**, **M**, **NG**) as syllables, with the result that a word such as "insutanto" (the Japanese version of "instant") will sound like a six-syllable word to a Japanese! You can explain that an English syllable needs a vowel sound in the syllable. The most practical solution to this and other confusions is to use tapping exercises until your students intuitively perceive syllables in an English sense.

Despite what would appear to be a worrisome variety of reasons for people not to get the point right away, most students do pick up the idea of syllables rapidly. The concept is repeated regularly in the following units.

Hand tapping

Some students are reluctant to tap their desks to demonstrate the number of syllables. Although some kind of physical marking is needed to truly grasp the sense of syllable rhythm, there are various ways to remove any embarrassment from the activity. Students can tap a pencil or, for more privacy, they can tap their knees under the desk or simply touch thumb to little finger to mark the syllable beat, or tap a foot.

Psychological resistance

If a student resists even this covered or invisible motion, it may be that there is a fundamental undercurrent of resistance to changing rhythm at all. Students sometimes have psychological barriers to "sounding foreign," and this makes them resist unconsciously. Pronunciation is far more apt to activate this kind of reluctance than drilling in more psychologically neutral aspects of language, such as grammar or vocabulary. After all, we learn the rhythm of our native language long before we learn to say words, and it is part of our sense of who we are and where we belong. For this reason, it is wise for the teacher to notice resistance and not to meet it head on but to gradually coax the students along to the new rhythm.

If limericks and other related activities are amusing and relaxed, their use can go a long way in helping to lower the "affective filter" of unconscious resistance. The technique of Pair Practice can also greatly facilitate this process because it not only demonstrates the practical usefulness of saying the remark in an English way but it also reinforces the idea that all the students are working together toward reasonable goals.

B

Pair practice

Pair Practice exercises should take about 10 minutes, but class quickness varies a great deal. In general, you should halt the exercise when a majority of the pairs have finished going through the list of challenges. If there is a general eagerness to continue by running through the challenges again, you can give more time. If the exercise is too easy for your particular students, it is best to cut the number of items in half or to eliminate the exercise entirely.

Pair activities can be conducted in different ways, but in general the following procedures should be followed:

1. Students should have the opportunity to read the sentences first before beginning the Pair Practice.
2. Partners should take turns being Student 1 and Student 2. Remind them not to always choose the first or second sentence, but to make this a real challenge for the listener.
3. Partners should be changed from time to time to add variety to the practice. If possible, students should have different first languages.
4. You should walk around and listen. Rather then correct on the spot, some teachers prefer not to correct on the spot but to save notes to give feedback to the whole class at the end of the exercise. This keeps the students' attention focused on their responsibility to listen to each other. On the other hand, circulating among

pairs gives you an unusually good opportunity to give personal attention to each student. Therefore, you may find correction on the spot is best.
5. For variety, you or one student can be Student 1, with the whole class being Student 2. Alternatively, the Pair Practice can be used as a quiz.

C

Counting syllables in a sentence

Procedure

Students should work alone on the number of syllables and then practice them in pairs or compare their answers with a partner or with the class.

Answers

1. Buy a washing machine.   6
2. Where is the electrical panel?   9
   (If "Where is" is contracted, there will be one less syllable, but contractions have not been taught yet, so the student cannot be expected to know that.)
3. Do we need a garage mechanic?   9
4. Students in school must study.   7
5. Computer programming is a good profession.   12
6. Automobile parts are made in many countries.   12
7. They closed the department store in August.   10
8. We rented it before noon.   7

D

Pair practice: sentences

Pair practice error correction

If a student makes an error beyond what is being practiced in the pair of sentences, it is important for the partner to learn to ask for a clarification.

For instance, in sentence 8a, Student 1 might say "What does *crackéd* mean?" (adding a syllable where it is not appropriate). Student 2 should ask "Do you mean cracked?" If Student 2 does not notice the error, you can step in and ask the question.

Spelling

At moments when there is difficulty with communication, it is helpful to be able to spell clearly, but a surprising number of advanced students are not able to say all the letters of the alphabet correctly. Common errors are with the letters "a," "e," "g," "i," and "j." Unless the control is automatic, spelling the problem word will just compound the communication difficulty. This is the time for students to discover alphabet weaknesses. One way to uncover this on the very first day of class is to ask students to dictate the spelling of their names. Write on the board exactly what you hear even if you can guess that the student mean a different letter. This makes the error immediately apparent; it also has the advantage of introducing class members to each other and helping you to learn their names quickly.

E

Grammar: the past tense 🔲

Some of your students, especialy those from Southeast Asia, may speak languages that do not normally have consonants at the end of words. They may feel the teacher is simply being fussy in reminding them to pay attention to final consonants. This type of exercise can help motivate students to sharpen their final consonants by making clear the grammatical significance of the presence or absence of these sounds.

Demonstration techniques

You can erase the dropped letter or draw a line through it. If there's time for preparation, the "Vanishing Letters" technique is an intriguing way to display the difference between a past tense verb with or without an added syllable. Make a poster listing some of the following verbs, but write the silent letter with a yellow marker (any color can be used for the other letters). Show this poster and then cover it with a red acetate screen. You can use half of a clear red report cover, obtained from a stationery store, as the screen. The yellow letters will disappear behind the red screen. This technique can be used in an- other context, as explained on page 31 of Unit 12.

Answers

Past tense	Syllables	Past tense	Syllables
painted	2	opened	2
rented	2	closed	1
needed	2	liked	1
wanted	2	disliked	2
decided	3	cleaned	1
selected	3	returned	2
visited	3	worked	1
represented	4	called	1
intended	3	practiced	2

F

Pair practice

If your students are enrolled in a full English course, this practice will reinforce the grammar lessons. If pronunciation is their only class subject (for instance, in a workplace class), they may initially find focusing on abstractions about grammar difficult. In either case, the purpose of this exercise is to remind students in a practical way that the number of syllables has an effect on meaning.

G

Dropped syllables 🔲

Extra words such as "temperature, evening, accidentally, aspirin, favorite" could be assigned as dictionary homework.

H
Dictation 📼

If you are not using the cassettes, read these sentences aloud two times. Read the complete sentence, not dictating word by word but in thought groups, such as "Vegetables are expensive/at the present time." If the dictations seem too easy, increase the challenge by requiring students to keep the entire sentence in memory; that is, do not read only a phrase or thought group. You can also increase the challenge by reading more quickly and with more reduction.

Students should be encouraged to take dictation on the board as much as possible because this helps them recognize errors instantly. Dictation on paper can be checked by having students exchange papers with a partner. Another good approach is to have students dictate to each other; this emphasizes both speaking and listening. To avoid arguments over who was "at fault," it is best to wait until the class has developed a sense of mutual responsibility.

Correcting

Spelling errors are not important here; what is important is the students' awareness of syllable number. The best way to check this is to ask for a count and to have the students read aloud. If the vocabulary is too difficult for your students, choose a simpler text, one that contains past tense verbs and other words that may cause syllable number difficulty. The most common problem is inserting a vowel into a consonant cluster (e.g. prayed/parade).

Answers

1. Vegetables are expensive at the present time.   12
2. They walked to the store to buy chocolate.   9
3. He works in an interesting business.   9
4. We recorded everything and waited for the results.   14
5. I opened the closet and laughed at what I saw.   12

I
Check your progress

The words "this is" may cause overcorrection, with too much emphasis to a word ("is") that should normally be de-emphasized. That possibility is justified at this point in the course because of the importance of getting students to "feel" the presence of a syllable. No matter how unstressed or short a syllable is, it must still be present.

J
Syllable number game

Amusing activities are valuable in the pronunciation class because they lower tension. This game should take about 10 minutes at most: 5 minutes for teams to make their lists and 5 minutes for putting them on the board and assigning points. An especially lively version of this game (provided by Carole Mawson) is to send the teams to the board, each member with a piece of chalk. Under columns labeled 1, 2 and 3, they write as many words as they can. When time is up, team members read their lists aloud. The rest of the class looks for mistakes in spelling or syllable number. A misspelled word gets no point, but a word in the wrong column gets a point taken off the team score. Students often want to continue the game with another topic to list, but it is usually best to finish on a high note.

Stops and continuants

The perfection trap

Serious students and teachers alike have a tendency to wish to work at individual sound problems "until they are mastered" before continuing with the course. The problem with this attitude is that it delays work on rhythm. Research suggests that target language sounds can be improved more efficiently if spoken in the target language rhythm (Abberton, et al. 1978). For example, Spanish sounds are not easily made clear if spoken with a Portuguese rhythm, and English sounds are extra difficult if spoken with a Japanese rhythm.

An even more serious reason why you should not allow yourself or your students to be caught in the perfection trap was explained clearly by Joan Morley:

> At best, perfectionistic performance goals turn out to be unrealistic; at worst, they can be devastating: They can defeat students who feel they cannot measure up, and they can frustrate teachers who feel they have failed in their job. (1991: 498)

Therefore, the best approach is to present the material, give the students a chance to absorb the concepts and practice them, and then move on. Reassure students that these sounds will occur repeatedly throughout the course and that improvement will be aided by work on English rhythm.

Confusion pairs

Some of the pairs of sounds presented in Unit 2 are not the "confusion pairs" you may be used to, such as **R** and **L**. The reason is that students need to concentrate on the feature being taught (in this case, stops versus continuants). For instance, the **S/T** contrast was chosen to begin the lesson for the very reason that few language groups would have trouble with the contrast. **R, L, V,** and **B** are introduced separately rather than in the usual pairings in order to focus the students' minds on the teaching point of the unit rather than reactivating what may be a long-practiced sense of discouragement. Put another way, the sound distinctions are being approached from a different angle. Here is an example of a sound confusion that depends on the stop/continuant contrast: "will defect/will affect."

S and T

One graphic way to demonstrate the difference between stops and continuants is to say the word "bus," continuing the **S** sound while walking back and forth in front of the class. You can continue such a sound as long as you still have air in your lungs. Now say the word "but." Then stop, holding up the palm of your hand facing the class in the nearly universal symbol for "Stop!" You can continue the **S** but you must stop the **T**.

Take the time to encourage all students to try out the sounds silently while looking at the illustrations. They need to feel the placement of their tongues before making any attempt to say the words. Silent practice is important because it is difficult to feel a sound if you are saying it out loud; the auditory sensations tend to mask the physical sensations. This silent practice should not be rushed.

In silent practice, the final **T** in "but" should be held long enough for students to feel the placement of the tongue as it seals off the air flow. Emphasize the fact that the **T** is silent even when they say the word out loud. In North American spoken English, **T, P,** and **K** at the end of words are silent and "unreleased." No puff of air or vowel-type sound should follow "but," "cup," or "buck."

Once students have a physical sense of the difference between stops and continuants, the contrast can be used to clarify a number of sound problems. The North American R is difficult for Japanese, Spanish, Arabic, and other speakers because the sound is made in their languages with some kind of contact of the tip of the tongue against the roof of the mouth. This is also common in some British dialects. It can cause confusion in a North American context, however, because the native speaker automatically interprets it as a brief stop, much like the they way the letter "t" is pronounced in "city" or "beautiful." From the other direction, learners of English are apt to have trouble correctly distinguishing and identifying "a date" and "a rate."

Mouth illustrations

Many students are helped by a picture of the mouth making a sound, but some are confused when they first see such a picture. You can help them get oriented by drawing a profile on the board while they watch. It does not matter how anatomically accurate your picture is if you mention each part (eye, nose, lip) as the chalk line moves. Orientation is improved if you ask students to run their tongue-tip over the part you are drawing, especially the inside of the upper lip, front and back of the upper teeth, the tooth ridge and then back as far as they can reach. Then ask them to continue following the profile in this way as you draw the lower lip and teeth. Since this activity is entirely private, there is usually a high level of participation. No matter how unrealistic your sketch is, the students are getting a direct kinesthetic relationship to the drawing. This tongue-tip experience prepares them for later directions, such as "Press the sides of your tongue on the tooth ridge above your upper teeth on the sides of your mouth."

B
TH *and* T

Tongue-between-the-teeth sounds (interdental: **TH**) are rare in other languages. They may be embarrassing for some students to practice because of the feeling that it is impolite, even disgusting, to show one's tongue. Practicing with a small mirror can be helpful because it shows the student's tongue tip and prevents the mouth from being seen by others.

In general, it is important to be sensitive to students' embarrassment, which has such a constraining effect. An advantage of choral practice (i.e. having the whole class speak at once) is that privacy is preserved; students can feel free to experiment more or less anonymously. Of course, in choral recitation, it is more difficult for the teacher to monitor each student. That is why it works well to begin with choral practice and then go on to pair practice.

A, C, and D
Pair practice: words with **TH** *and* **T**/ sentences with **TH** *and* **T**

If you have a monolingual class, you may find that the Pair Practice exercises in Units 2–6 might not be effective. Students who speak the same language may give each other "clues" about the sound (such as making an extra effort on the difficult one) that the partner can recognize but which would be useless in conversation with a native speaker of English. For monolingual classes, it may be better to save pair practice activity for exercises that do not involve individual sounds, such as syllable number, stress, or sentence emphasis.

Some students may be substituting **S** for **TH** in these exercises. This confusion pair is presented in Unit 6, "Concentrating on sibilants," and also in

Appendix B, "Additional work on consonants." In this early point of the course, where the teaching focus is the contrast of stop versus continuant, it is better to be satisfied with the continuant **S** and wait to correct the error during later presentations of the contrast between **S** and **TH**.

E

R *and* D

The **R** sound can be practiced by holding a small piece of paper (perhaps an inch wide) in the mouth so that the roof of the mouth is mostly kept screened off from the tongue. The paper is a reminder not to let the tongue tip touch the roof of the mouth while saying **R**. Keeping the paper in place, try saying **D**. The feel of the paper makes clear the way the tongue must press against the tooth ridge all the way around to make this stop sound. The **R** should be made without touching the paper at all. *Note:* It is a good idea to try all techniques yourself before presenting them to a class.

H

Linking practice: R ▭

Most people learn a foreign language through their eyes by reading printed words. Because of this, learners often have great difficulty identifying words in the stream of speech; they are expecting to see spaces in between the words. The fact is, the only people who speak with "spaces" are language teachers trying to be helpful.

Beginning students of French are always taught about "liaison," the way words run together. This is considered essential for the production of understandable spoken French and for listening comprehension. Unfortunately, students of English are usually not taught the same way, despite the fact that English also runs words together. Both speech clarity and listening comprehension are limited by ignorance of linking

because the learner is easily confused about where the words end. The listener, expecting word separations, will have trouble recognizing individual words. The words "an ice" could be heard as "a nice." Or "all of," when linked together, might make the learner believe that "a love" was meant. This is an error that would completely throw the listener off track because it wouldn't make sense. A native speaker of English would not make this mistake because the context would be clear. But the learner of English is struggling with many listening problems, and the presence of linking adds to the difficulty.

Demonstration techniques

The following two techniques are based on the principle that the difficulty of *reading* run-together words mimics the difficulty of *hearing* run-together words.

1. **Sliding words**   Get a clear plastic report cover (or a sheet of transparency film) and a piece of white cardboard from a stationery store. Fold the white cardboard to make a standing easel for your display. If you have the plastic slide binder from the report cover, you can use it as a base for the front edge of the easel. Cut the report cover or transparency film into two or four rectangles, depending upon how big you want the words to be. With a black marker write HI on one piece of the clear plastic and THERE on another. Now you can push these two pieces into the slide binder on your easel. Slide them together so that they spell HITHERE. Present the easel display to your students and ask them to guess the pronunciation of HITHERE. This is an ambiguous word that could be read as HI THERE or as HIT HERE. (See Figure 1.) You could also use ISIT (which could mean I SIT or IS IT?) or ATALL (which could mean A TALL or AT ALL). The meaning is unclear until you slide the pieces apart so that a space appears between the words. The space makes the words clear.

Figure 1 **Sliding words**

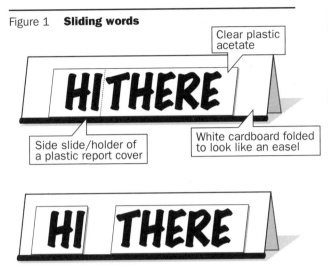

Clear plastic acetate

Side slide/holder of a plastic report cover

White cardboard folded to look like an easel

2. **Folded sentences** (idea provided by Elina Holst)   Print words such as A TALL or GO OUT on a sheet of paper, then make a pleat in the paper so that the space between the words is eliminated. Present the resulting "strange word" to the students. After they have had time to be puzzled, stretch the paper out, making the meaning clear. (See Figure 2.) This technique is also effective for

Figure 2 **Folded sentences**

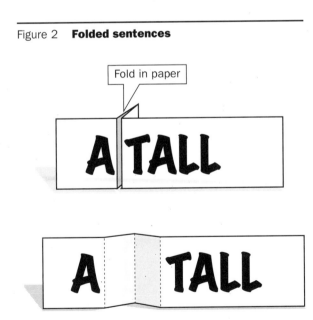

Fold in paper

presenting silent letters such as vowels ("closed," Unit 1) and the **H** in pronouns ("Is he," Unit 12).

J

Rhythm practice: **R** *and* **D** 🔲

The short poems in the Student's Book can be used to alter the pace of class work. Limericks and other light poetry are used as often as possible in the text to take advantage of the way the swing of the rhythm forces reductions and contractions. This rhythmic swing will be broken if students have to pause at each line to figure out which words to emphasize. It is better to have them read the poem first to themselves and underline the emphasized words before oral practice. One useful approach is to assign the poems as homework. If students have memorized the words, they will be able to recite without the struggle involved in reading out loud. This will encourage a more rhythmic and less monotone recitation.

By beginning with a choral reading, no individual is put on the spot. Each half of the class can alternate reading lines out loud. If you act as choral leader, clapping a strong rhythmic pattern or thumping your hand on the table, the class will stay together in a satisfying way. Without this leadership, the rhythm is apt to become uncertain, and that might make your students uneasy.

The poems can be presented in a variety of ways, depending on the atmosphere in your particular classroom. Emphatic beats can be marked by group "upper body movement" gestures (Acton 1991: 3). The more lively and playful the rendition, the better. The more students actually *move*, the more they will feel the essential rhythm of English, and the more freely they will be able to express that rhythm in their speech. Singing popular songs is a good extension of the limerick-type activities, but care must be taken in choosing lyrics that are understandable and actually fit the rhythm of spoken English.

K

Check your progress: dictation 🔲

Play the cassette or dictate the following sentences using the contracted form "We're" in the first sentence to begin to get the students used to hearing contractions. When checking what students have written, accept either full or contracted forms as long as the target sound is correct. Also, since it is necessary to concentrate the students' minds on the teaching point of the unit (the difference between stops and continuants), other issues (such as spelling) should be temporarily ignored.

Answers

1. We're almost ready.
2. Thank you for all your help
3. They paid Ann very well for the work.
4. Math is a difficult subject for us.
5. Are all our cards here?

Review

Number of syllables

Answers

X: Maybe we planned to do too much.	8
Y: Yes, but I wanted to see more.	8
X: You were the one who decided to stop.	10
Y: Well, I needed to rest.	6
X: And I wanted to continue!	8

More stops and continuants: grammar

A

Pair practice with R and D: past or present?

This exercise introduces students to the fact that the final sound has grammatical meaning. This is particularly important for those students who have a tendency to leave off final consonants. It is also important practice for students who have difficulty with listening comprehension. The small difference between hearing a stop or a continuant can make a major difference in understanding what was said.

Use the Pair Practice activity only to the extent that it is needed. If your students are doing these exercises easily, either skip the exercise entirely or shorten it.

B

Pair practice with D and continuants: past or present?

Students may not be making clear sounds with **S** and **Z**. In Unit 6 they will study the difference between these sounds and also **SH**. At this point in the course, it is important for students simply to concentrate on the stop/continuant difference.

C

Pair practice with S and stops: singular or plural?

This exercise is particularly important for students who have a tendency to omit plural or third person singular endings.

D

Linking practice: continuants

If a sound is particularly difficult, practicing it in the linking position can help focus the students' attention. Sometimes the sound is said more easily in the final position; continuing it into the initial position of the next word can increase control in that position.

E

Linking practice: stops

Students often have trouble identifying the end of one word and the beginning of another. This is particularly true when a stop sound "moves over" to begin the next word, as quite commonly occurs in normal English speech.

F

V and B

It is important that students press the *inner* part of the lower lip against the *front* of the upper teeth. If the teeth are touching the outer part of the lower lip, the sound will be more like **B**, a common result of Japanese efforts to make a **V**. If the teeth aren't actually pressing the lip, the **V** will sound like a **W**, a common problem for East Indians. One technique that may help is to ask students to identify pairs of **B** and **V** words while you are *whispering* the words.

I

Linking practice: V and B

Students are asked to draw linking marks before they say the sentences because this is a kinesthetic way to focus their minds on the principle of linking.

J

Pair practice: dialogue 🔲

Students can practice the dialogue in the relative privacy of pair practice. However, if there is a playful atmosphere in the class, this activity can be done by a pair reading while the class listens. The more emotional content there is in the reading, the better. To get this playacting atmosphere started, you might take the part of "Y" first, putting a tone of self-pity into the lines.

M

L *and* D

Many of your students may have trouble distinguishing between **R** and **L**. The distinction between these two sounds is addressed in Appendix B. However, at this point in the course, it is important to keep your students' attention focused directly on the difference between stops and continuants. Therefore, **R** is contrasted only with **D** (Unit 2 and 3), and **L** is contrasted only with **D** (Unit 3). When students understand that it is necessary to lower the tongue position (except for the tip) for **L** in order to allow air to flow out continuously, they will find it easier to compare this tongue position with the bunched up shape of **R**. If most of the students in your class need help with this, show them the comparison tongue drawings on page 124 of the Student's Book.

O

Check your progress: dictation 🔲

Play the cassette or read these sentences aloud.

Answers
1 We share all our work.
2. She joined every club that interested her.
3. I rushed around to get ready on time.
4. Bring a book to read because the trains are always late.
5. They saved all five of our old letters.
6. We believe everything you tell us.

4 Rhythm: stops and syllable length

This course began the study of rhythm with syllable counting (Unit 1). Rhythm is now reintroduced by practicing the effect of the stop/continuant contrast on the length of the preceding vowel (Peterson and Lehiste 1967: 200). Since most ESL/EFL students automatically transfer their customary rhythm patterns to the new language, vigorous attention must be given to substituting new rhythm patterns.

People learn the rhythm of language in infancy and thereafter apply it unconsciously to their own language or to any other language they are learning. Because of the central importance of learning English rhythm, the subject is spiraled throughout most of the units.

Demonstration technique: using a rubber band

> The heart of the rhythmic system–syllable length–may be initially difficult for students to apprehend through the ear but may be more clearly demonstrated through the use of the other senses. (Wong 1987: 25)

Stretching wide, heavy rubber bands while practicing the lengthened vowels can provide students with a kinesthetic focusing tool to reinforce the contrast in duration. The use of rubber bands is especially helpful for students whose own language rhythm is based on the equal length of syllables (e.g., in Spanish, Japanese, and many other languages). Thin bands are apt to break and also do not give the full impression of the effort involved in making some syllables longer than others.

Long/short

Some teachers may object to using the words "long" and "short" to describe the actual length of the vowels because these words are often used to describe the sound quality of vowel pairs such as those vowels in "ship/sheep" or "pull/pool." It is true that it would be better not to use the same terms for different purposes. However, the terms "long" and "short" help the student produce authentic English rhythm because they are precisely accurate to the duration contrasts students must learn.

C
Rhythm practice

Whispering is a good alternative method for practicing many exercises. In this particular exercise, whispering the poem concentrates the mind on timing rather on than pitch patterns.

G
Listening practice with D and L: full or contracted?

This exercise is the first explicit presentation of contractions. It is presented as listening practice in order to allay student anxiety about contractions and reductions. It is common for students to worry about learning any form of reduction because they suspect that this is sloppy speech for uneducated people, and they also feel that some information is missing. These feelings, whether conscious or not, form a barrier to learning.

It is not helpful to meet this resistance with repeated corrections, no matter how well meant, as students are apt to resist pressure in a direction they fear. Therefore, it is far better and less threatening to introduce the topic as "useful for listening comprehension" and reassure students that they do not need to use reductions when they speak. In fact, it is better if they speak slowly when they really need to be understood, and reductions sound peculiar in slow speech. However, they must learn to *hear* reductions easily since most native English speakers use contractions and reductions when they speak.

Students soon begin to realize that contractions are part of the reason native speakers seem to "speak too fast." Failure to identify auxiliaries and pronouns is particularly damaging to listening comprehension. Therefore, it is useful for students to practice saying contractions and reductions to help "train their ears."

Contractions and reductions are spiraled throughout the course. By the time the students have completed the units on the Basic Emphasis Pattern (Units 11 and 12) and focus words (Units 13 and 14), they will understand why contractions and reductions are a systematic part of English when it is spoken at a normal rate of speed. This understanding encourages students to use contractions themselves. Even if they continue to speak in full forms, however, students will have greatly improved their listening comprehension.

Formal versus informal English

Tell students that reductions, including contractions, are not used in formal written English, such as business letters and reports. Contractions convey an informality, mimicking speech, which is not appropriate for formal writing.

Demonstration technique

One way to present contractions visually is to show students two pieces of paper. One has the word "she" on it and the other has the word "is." Now bring the pieces of paper together so that they overlap and the "i" in "is" is covered. This approximates the way these two words are usually spoken. You could use a whole set of contractions for this demonstration.

Answers

Play the cassette or read the following sentences aloud.

1. b.	They'd ask a good question.	would
2. a.	He'll answer soon.	will
3. b.	We'd prefer to pay cash.	would
4. b.	Do you think they'd like it?	would
5. a.	I said I'll do the work.	will
6. b.	Who'd they ask?	did
7. b.	Where'd Ann find one?	did
8. a.	Perhaps he'll agree.	will
9. b.	Do you suppose she'd come?	would
10. a.	Where'll you put it?	will

Extended practice for Exercise G

Advanced students can be asked to write their own sentence pairs in which the verb stays the same while the sounds of contracted auxiliaries – **V**, **D**, and **L** – are all that indicate the tense. Give them the following list of verbs:

let	hurt	spread	hit	shut
cut	quit	cost	put	wet

Review

Dictation: stops and continuants 🔲

Play the cassette or read these sentences with the contractions. Accept either the contracted or the full form in the students' writing. This dictation tests both the stop/continuant distinction and syllable number. It also requires students to recognize the contracted forms. Because students are being asked to concentrate on these particular teaching points, spelling errors should be ignored.

Answers

1. She'd always asked interesting questions.
2. When they'd answered all her questions, they left.
3. He'll ask for a new book.
4. What's in the cart?
5. Who's going to pay cash?

Voicing

Kansas City Mice

This is a true story. At an engineering conference in Kansas City, two Americans took a colleague from Zurich to dinner. The Swiss engineer had rented a car and driven around the area the day before. This was the dialogue at dinner:

1st American: So, what have you found most interesting about Kansas City?

Swiss: The most interesting? It is the mice.

1st American: (*thinking of the hotel where they are staying*) Mice!?

Swiss: Yes, that is clear. Here are *much* mice.

2nd American: You mean ... *rodents*?

Swiss: (*being unfamiliar with the term, is silent*)

1st American: You've *seen* them?

Swiss: Oh yes, I saw them myself, all around the city.

2nd American: (*trying a different approach, holds hands a mouse-length and then a rat-length apart*) Would you say they are *this* big or *that* big?

Swiss: (*holding one hand high above his head*) No, not that. *This* big!

The two Americans then realized that their Swiss colleague meant "corn." The term "maize" (which rhymes with "days") is used in British English, but is not commonly used in North America, although a popular corn oil for cooking is named "Mazola." When "maize" is spoken with a German rendering of the letters "ai" and with a devoiced final consonant, according to German usage, the word comes out "mice."

This conversation was only temporarily derailed because the goodwill among the colleagues encouraged them to make the effort to get the discussion back on track.

The main point of this unit is for students to learn that two contrasting sounds can be made with the tongue in exactly the same position, but with a contrast in voicing. Although many languages use voicing contrasts, the concept needs to be taught because it does not always transfer easily to the new language. This lesson may take extra time because so many sound problems can be traced to the voicing distinction.

In a study of errors made by speakers of English as a second language (Leahy 1980), it was found that the two principal types of errors were based on voicing (buzz/bus) and continuancy (bus/but).

In voicing errors, the problem with stop sounds was found to be mainly in the final position (cab/cap) and was directly related to the length of the preceding vowel (see Unit 7). The voicing errors with continuants occurred in all positions, not just in the final position (sink/zinc, ether/either, bus/buzz). Some languages, such as German, tend to devoice any final voiced stop (**D**, **D**, **G**), and this can compound a syllable number confusion, producing a substitution such as "plan it" for "planned."

Demonstration technique

For practice in learning to hear voicing differences while saying them, just covering the ears will not be adequate. Tell students to press their fingers *firmly* to close the ears in order to get the full effect of the contrast. The sound **Z** should not be pronounced "zee" (like the alphabet name of the letter) but should be continued as "Zzzz" (like a buzz). Similarly, the sound **S** should be continued as a hiss. The contrast is caused by the presence or absence of vibration of the vocal cords. Another way to help students to notice the vibration is by asking them to press a hand lightly to their throat while alternating between "Zzzz" and "Ssss." It is then possible to feel the vibration. Try this out yourself first to determine which demonstration method, closing the ears or touching the throat, seems to work best.

The voicing feature is a good way to help identify a difficult sound. Present an unfamiliar word such as "grisly" (pronounced with a voiced **Z** sound). Ask the students if the "s" letter is voiced or unvoiced. Despite the spelling, the sound is voiced. The word "grisly" was chosen because it is almost certain to be unknown, but you may want to use a more common word. When the students have learned to recognize the difference between voiced and unvoiced sounds, this feature is an analytical tool for clearly hearing and mentally recording the pronunciation of a new word.

Write these sounds on the board: **F TH T S K P**
Ask for the voiced partner: **V TH D Z G B**

It may help to present the contrasts in nonsense syllables (fay/vay, etc.). Because it is difficult to show the voicing difference for **TH** without phonetic symbols, you can draw a wavy line under **TH** to show voicing:

Unvoiced	Voiced
thank	then

Extended practice

If more work is needed, have the students dictate to each other from lists of words in this lesson, choosing the voiced or unvoiced version at random. The partner writes what was heard. This gives immediate feedback on the clarity of the distinction. If your students all speak the same language, this type of dictation will not work well.

A
S *and* Z

2 Answers
(The underlined word is different.)

1. Sue	Sue	<u>zoo</u>	3
2. bus	<u>buzz</u>	bus	2
3. sink	sink	<u>zinc</u>	3
4. peace	<u>peas</u>	peace	2
5. <u>ice</u>	eyes	eyes	1
6. rise	rise	<u>rice</u>	3

Concentrating on sibilants

A

Sibilants

Many languages do not have a **TH** sound, and sibilants are sometimes the substitute sound. **TH** is not a sibilant, and therefore, understanding the distinctive feature of sibilance can help clarify the **TH**. Other problems can be aided by understanding the feature of sibilance. For instance, Japanese students sometimes have difficulty making a pronoun clear because English listeners misunderstand "he" as "she." The problem does not come from a grammar error, but from the way Japanese phonological rules tend to add sibilance to **H**, causing the English listener to assume **SH** must have been intended.

To distinguish **S** from **SH**, start from the **S** position and then draw back the tongue a short distance, keeping the sides of the tongue in contact with the tooth ridge. The tip of the tongue no longer touches the lower teeth. Remind students to round their lips for **SH**. If your students are having trouble distinguishing "he" and "she," tell them to lower their tongues a little for "he" so that they don't cause sibilance.

If students are having trouble distinguishing **S** from **TH**, point out that **S** is a sibilant and **TH** is not. In **TH**, the tongue is relaxed and flat so that the airflow lacks the hissing characteristic of sibilants. Sibilance is the result of high velocity turbulance of the air flowing through a narrow channel. Ask students to compare the width of the air flow arrow for the illustration of "**S** from above" on page 9 of the Student's Book with the picture of "**TH** from above" on page 10. The **S** arrow is quite narrow because the air is being forced through a narrow channel, which produces the high pitched sibilance. The **TH** arrow, on the other hand, is quite wide because the tongue is flat so that the air flow is not obstructed.

Some Asian students make **TH** with too little sound. They need to add more sound but not sibilance. Give these directions: Silently place your tongue in the **TH** position with the tip lightly touching the cutting edge of the lower teeth. Then breathe out and notice the low sound the air makes as it flows past the teeth. Now, keeping the tip in the same position, press the sides of the tongue upwards against the tooth ridge. This position leaves only a narrow valley along the middle of the tongue. Breathe out strongly and notice the high hissing noise that the air makes as it strikes the teeth.

C

SH/CH and J/Y

Some students have a problem hearing the difference between "chew," and "shoe." This "hearing difficulty" is often reflected in their speech and is caused by phonological rules in their own language. It can be helpful to approach the distinction between **CH** and **SH** as a contrast between a stop and a continuant. Phonetically speaking, **CH** and **J** are affricates, not stops, but from a practical point of view, calling them stops helps the students analyze the difference. It is more exact to say that the sound *begins* with a quick stop.

You can write the pair on the board and add some sort of "phonetic" spelling:

share / tshare (chair)
sheep / tsheep (cheap)

Just as you can write "share" and "tshare" on the board to show the pronunciation difference between "share" and "chair," it is possible to distinguish "yellow" and "Jell-o" by writing "yellow" and "dzhello." Spanish speakers often have trouble with this contrast. **J** is a sibilant because it is a combination of the **D** and **ZH** sounds. **ZH** is a sibilant produced by the hissing of air rushing through a narrow channel. **Y**, on the other hand, is not a sibilant because the air is spread out more across the top of the tongue, so there is no hissing. The contrast between **J** and **Y** can be practiced with tongue twisters such as:

The New York Jets yell "Yes" to Jell-o.

E

Sibilants and number of syllables: S, Z, SH, CH, and J 🔲

2 Answers
All of the words in columns B and D end in sibilants.

I

Dictation 🔲

Play the cassette or read these sentences aloud.

Answers
1. Please don't put ice in my water.
2. I heard that they're raising bees.
3. We've all watched that TV program.
4. Do you think you'll have enough rice?
5. She's asking for potato chips and Jell-o.

7 Rhythm: voicing and syllable length

Unit 7 reintroduces the theme of syllable length, this time in a different context in order to increase control of English rhythm.

It doesn't very often happen that a student *immediately* puts a lesson to good use, but the following story actually occurred. On Monday, a workplace class practiced vowel lengthening before a voiced sound. On Tuesday, a Nicaraguan member of the class called his garage to find out about the car he had left for repair. He said "Is Esteef there?" The mechanic said there was no such person at that number. The Nicaraguan thought back to the previous day's lesson and said, carefully lengthening the vowel, "Is Esteeef there?" Although the Spanish pattern still produced an extra syllable and de-voiced the final sound, the mechanic was now able to understand the request and said, "Oh, you mean *Steve!*" Business could then proceed. On Wednesday, the Nicaraguan reported this incident to the class, reinforcing Monday's lesson with a considerable tone of triumph. This was a happy day for the teacher.

Another illustration of this problem with vowel length before voicing occurred when an American student told her new Dutch friend that he was very good at math. He answered proudly, "Yes, I'm a real wiskit." There was a long pause while she considered that he might have said "biscuit." Unfortunately, this made no sense. She finally figured out that he had meant "whiz kid," and they were able to continue the conversation.

B
Listening practice 🔲

Answers
(The underlined word is different.)

1. have	have	<u>half</u>	C
2. teeth	teeth	<u>teethe</u>	C
3. <u>leaf</u>	leave	leave	A
4. save	<u>safe</u>	save	B
5. batch	batch	<u>badge</u>	C
6. <u>Miss</u>	Ms.	Ms.	A
7. cap	cap	<u>cab</u>	C
8. back	<u>bag</u>	back	B

G
Words that end in stops 🔲

It is common for teachers to "finish" stop sounds at the end of words in order to help students hear better. Since most native English speakers do not complete these sounds, it is better not to give this "added clue." Students need to learn to depend on the clues that actually occur in normal speech.

I
Map game: "Oldtimer and Newcomer"

Photocopy the map on page 51 of the Student's Book, if students are sharing a book, so that everyone has a map. Give students time to practice the "useful phrases." You may want to add some to this list. Remind them that they may not use their hands to point at anything or to describe anything. This is a considerable constraint for most people because it requires them to depend entirely on language.

Although it is hard to estimate how much time to allow for this game (since it is generally quite popular and productive of language learning), you will probably need to plan for at least 15 to 20 minutes. Students recognize the usefulness of the exercise, and they also enjoy the total change of activity.

J

Dictation 🔊

Play the cassette or read these sentences aloud.

Answers

1. What kind of seat is this?
2. She rode as well as she could.
3. Who's about ready to leave?
4. He's looking for a yellow cab.
5. There's something in my ice and I don't like it!

Review

Number of syllables

Answers

Past tense	Number of syllables
started	2
rented	2
recorded	3
completed	3
stopped	1
saved	1
hoped	1
planned	1
judged	1
lifted	2

Plural or third person singular	Number of syllables
ices	2
juices	2
uses	2
judges	2
sentences	3
pleases	2
loves	1
believes	2
parades	2
fences	2
completes	2
trades	1
mixes	2
manages	3
freezes	2
saves	1
attaches	3
colleges	3

Stress: vowel length

Rhythm and stress

Stress has a critical effect on the rhythm of a sentence. Rhythm is not just something extra added to the basic sequence of consonants and vowels. It is a systematic guide to the structure of information in the spoken message (G. Brown 1977: 43).

The following is a scenario that actually occurred (supplied by Karen Yoshihara). A Japanese visitor to the United States needed a resistor for an electronic gadget, so he went to an electronics supply store and asked the clerk for a "**reg**ista." The clerk could not understand what he wanted. The customer, recognizing that there was something wrong with his pronunciation, tried again, this time carefully pronouncing the final consonant.

Customer: **Reg**ister?
Clerk: (*looking at the cash register*) Excuse me?
Customer: (*trying a change of vowel*) **Rah**gista?
Clerk: Sir?
Customer: (*deciding the problem was the sound* **J**) **Rah**zista!
Clerk: (*impatiently*) I'm sorry, we don't have anything like that.
Customer: (*furious*) Right here! Look at this picture! A **rah**zista!
Clerk: (*suddenly understanding*) Oh, you mean a re**sis**tor!

Importance of stress

Many students assume that word stress patterns are some sort of frill, or else they do not notice them at all. Far from being frills, stress patterns are an essential part of the pronunciation of English words. English speakers tend to store vocabulary according to stress patterns (Levelt 1989: 373). When the wrong pattern is heard, the listener may spend time searching stored words in the wrong category. By the time the listener realizes something is wrong, the original sequence of sounds may be forgotten. For this reason, a stress pattern mistake can cause great confusion, especially if it is accompanied by any other kind of error (G. Brown 1977: 43).

Errors in word stress are often a result of transfer from the learner's first language. For example, stress in Punjabi or Czech usually falls on the first syllable of a word, whereas stress in Hebrew usually falls on the last syllable.

Signals of stress

It has long been the practice to teach stress as if it were synonymous with loudness, but this approach may not be as useful as previously assumed. Anything which calls attention to a syllable gives the *impression* of loudness, and this effect is common in most languages. "Musical" signals, such as vowel lengthening or pitch change, are used in most languages but are not always used for the same functions or in the same combinations. For that reason, it is helpful to teach students the special ways English uses these musical elements.

The three most powerful signals for indicating stress in English are:

1. Length of vowel
2. Clarity of vowel
3. Pitch change

(Bolinger 1958; Fry 1955)

This course reserves pitch change for the signaling of emphasis at the level of a sentence, not for word stress (see Unit 13, "Focus 1: pitch patterns used for emphasis"). It is true that a word said alone will have a pitch pattern to help indicate which syllable is stressed; for example:

┐╴╴ ╴┌─┐╴
atom/atomic

The reason is that a word said in isolation is, in effect, a complete utterance. When that word is spoken in a sentence, the pitch change will not actually "come through" unless the word has particular significance in that sentence.

Pitch changes are so important in conveying the meaning of a sentence that this signal is not introduced until Unit 13, which begins the study of musical effects at the level of the sentence. Concentrating on length (rhythm) and clarity (reducing vowels) is enough for students to think about at this stage of the course.

Degrees of length

Basically, there are three lengths for vowels (the centers of syllables):

1. *Reduced* (**so**fa). This is the schwa sound, reduced in both clarity and length.
2. *Full vowel unstressed* (alteration). This is the full sound, not lengthened.
3. *Full vowel stressed* (alte**ra**tion). This is the full sound, lengthened to make it noticeable.

These vowel lengths are not exact measurements, so there is no point in trying to reduce English to musical notation or in asking students to practice three-way timing contrasts. The purpose of the lesson is simply to increase the students' awareness of the irregularity of English syllables and the general principle that *length adds emphasis*. Length is a reliable marker of stress, and it is the signal that most students find easiest to control (Chela de Rodriguez 1991: 353).

Reduced vowels produce a different psychological effect. For that reason, the sign at the zoo saying "DON'T FEED BEARS" has "command power" in English because of the unusual succession of full vowels. If there are no reduced vowels, the rhythm sounds staccato. Portuguese, Russian, French, German, and some other languages have reduced vowels, but students whose native language is Spanish, Japanese, or Tagalog, for example, find reduced vowels a difficult concept.

Because of the different types of rhythm, it is difficult to compose a musically satisfying translation of poetry when going from an equal-syllable language (where syllables are more or less the same length) to an unequal-syllable language (such as English or Portuguese) or to translate in the opposite direction. When English is spoken without vowel reduction and other forms of variable syllable length, the English listener gets an impression of a staccatolike rhythm. This inappropriate rhythm pattern is a basic cause of "foreign accent" in English.

English rhythm is based not only on varying syllable lengths but also on sentence emphasis effects. The two levels (syllable timing and sentence accents) are very different. The main point about English rhythm is that the syllables are very unequal in length.

Length in different languages

Even if the student's first language has syllables of unequal length, the difference in length may be used for quite different purposes, and therefore, will not carry over in a useful way.

For example, vowel length makes a difference in meaning in some languages in the same way that "bit" and "bet" are different words in English.

Japanese examples:

oba-san	=	aunt
obaa-san	=	grandmother
biru	=	building
biiru	=	beer

In Japanese the high vowels (spelled with "i" and "u" in Roman letters) are de-voiced if they occur between unvoiced consonants or between an unvoiced consonant and silence (e.g., "sukiyaki"). Since English vowels are always voiced, the English listener has difficulty processing this de-voiced vowel and assumes that it was reduced or even dropped. Therefore, the English listener is apt to hear the Japanese name "Takeshita" as three syllables or the word "desu" as one syllable.

Just as Japanese may lengthen vowels to express a "double vowel," Czech and Hungarian have vowel distinctions based on length. In Czech, the stress is almost always on the first syllable. However, there are long vowels that are marked with what we think of as a stress mark, but they may or may not be the stressed vowel.

Examples (both words are stressed on the first syllable):

kava   =   coffee
banán   =   banana

For native speakers of such languages, it is easy to hear vowel length difference but hard to associate this length with stress, which is its basic function in English.

If certain syllables are not reduced, the essential contrast between long and short is obscured. It is not enough to stress the word correctly; care must be taken also to *unstress* it correctly (McNerny and Mendelsohn 1992: 187).

The following confusion occurred during an ESL class in the workplace. A student took the teacher aside for private advice.

Student: Mrs. Stiebel, can you help me with comedy?
Teacher: Comedy?
Student: Yes, comedy is *big* problem.
Teacher: I don't quite follow.
Student: (*patiently*) Problem – that is *worry*.

Teacher: Yes, a worry. Um ... you mean you have a problem with comedy on TV?
Student: TV? (*tries again*) The boss put me on department comedy. Everybody on comedy, all the time argue.
Teacher: Oh, you mean *committee!*
Student: Yes, what I told you, comedy.

Techniques for teaching word stress

Use students' names or the names of cities in their countries. A long name such as "Yokohama" or "Acapulco" is especially good for demonstrating the uneven length of syllables that is characteristic of English. You can show how English speakers typically lengthen the next-to-last syllable in an unknown word (abraca**da**bra). Thus, an English speaker is apt to transfer the rhythm pattern of "banana" when saying the Spanish word "mañana." You can use dots and dashes, rubber bands, or short and long colored rods to represent successive syllables. Students can move the rods or other short and long markers around on their desks to represent the patterns of different words.

Sentence rhythm

Besides stress, which affects vowel length at the level of the syllable, there are lengthening effects at the sentence level. Because English depends so much on stress to highlight the important words in a sentence (see Unit 11), length affects more than just syllable rhythm. Lengthening of the stressed syllable in the word with the most emphasis is joined with pitch change to call attention to the speaker's main intent (see Unit 13). It may be that the purpose of lengthening this syllable is to give the listener time to notice which word is being highlighted. Contrasts of syllable length are presented in various ways during these early units in order to lay the foundation for later concepts critical to clear communication.

C

Listening for full and reduced vowels 🖙

Answers

1.	Soap gets out dirt fast.	All full
2.	All soap makes clothes clean.	All full
3.	Some soaps are better than others.	Mixed
4.	Those young men work hard.	All full
5.	All the women are working.	Mixed
6.	Toothpaste makes teeth white.	All full
7.	The toothpaste she uses is expensive.	Mixed
8.	Airplanes need good runways.	All full
9.	Many vowels are reduced in English.	Mixed
10.	Reduced vowels are harder to hear.	Mixed

F

Pair practice: abbreviations

Extended practice

Ask students to think of abbreviations and then use them in the same pair practice pattern "What does ... mean?" As a prompt, ask students if they know the abbreviations of universities such as UCLA (University of California Los Angeles), UBC (University of British Columbia), CCNY (City College of New York), other services or agencies, such as CPR (Canadian Pacific Railway), or locally familiar abbreviations.

Summary on length

The most important feature of English rhythm is that some syllables are longer than others.

Stress: vowel clarity

It ought to come as good news to the students that they do not have to pronounce every sound clearly and, indeed, they should not. Spoken English depends upon the effect produced by reducing vowel sounds to schwa. This is the one English sound that all learners must be made aware of at a very early stage—the neutral vowel used in unstressed syllables (Kenworthy 1987: 51).

Schwa is the most common vowel sound in English, but because it has no written form, it creates an immense barrier to listening comprehension for those who have studied English through print. At the same time, schwa is a barrier to learning to read for those who have learned English by listening. For these reasons, teaching conscious awareness of schwa can be a great help to students.

Schwa is both shortened (reduced) and muffled in quality (unclear). We use the words "reduced" and "unclear" in order to focus attention on both its shortness and its muffled quality. The phonetic symbol is ə. You might find it useful to teach your students to recognize this symbol when you write it above a word such as

    ə   ə
banana

Or you can simply use a slash over these reduced vowels (both methods are shown in the Student's Book).

Conscientious teachers tend to enunciate every sound clearly in order to help their students understand. They pronounce the unstressed syllables just as clearly as the stressed syllables. In fact, this is a kind of English that native English speakers use only when talking to nonnative speakers and children. The unfortunate effect of using such a model of spoken English is that students find it difficult to understand normal spoken English.

They become dependent upon clear and distinct pronunciation of all vowels and consonants instead of learning to listen for the information provided by stress contrasts (G. Brown 1977: 46).

Many languages are very careful to preserve the sound of each vowel in its full form. That is why English vowel reduction is so difficult for most English learners. On the other hand, if English is spoken with all vowels full, stress patterns become confused for the English listener. One technique is to say a word with all the vowels in full form, then with correct combinations of full and reduced vowels. Students can then practice saying the word both ways to feel the difference.

Extended activities

You can use "chocolate" again as an additional example (see the discussion for Unit 1). In many languages, every vowel in this word will be full. In English, the second vowel is either reduced or completely missing. Students' names can also be analyzed from the perspective of vowel clarity. Compare the typical English pronunciation, which is apt to reduce most of the vowels except for the next to last, as in "Yokohama." Russian is a language that also reduces unstressed vowels [e.g., "pravda" (truth)], but this doesn't necessarily transfer accurately to English. For instance, a Russian speaker is apt to say "San Francisco" with a reduction of the final vowel to schwa, which is not the way most residents of that city would say it.

Demonstration technique

Write "woman" and "women" on the board. Ask students which vowel sound changes, the first or the second. At least some students are likely to say it is the second. Now remind them that you asked about the vowel sound, not the spelling. Ask them to use their ears, not their eyes, and to listen for the difference between full and reduced vowels. Say the words again several times. Despite the spelling, the second vowel sounds roughly the same in each case, as it is reduced to schwa.

Added refinement

After you have practiced the exercises contrasting clear and unclear vowels, point out that the words "the" and "a" are spoken differently according to whether they are followed by a vowel or a consonant. This is done for the same reason that "a" changes to "an" before a vowel (e.g., "a pear," "an apple") because it is easier for an English speaker to say.

the plum	the apple
the pear	the orange
the decision	the election
a plum	an apple

B
Listening practice: identifying schwa 🔊

1 clear vowel	2 clear vowels
problem	mathematics
printed	economics
drama	economy
extra	photography
computer	absolute
employment	application
requirement	international

F
Word rhythm/sentence rhythm 🔊

1. attractive	It's active.
2. absolute	Have some fruit.
3. responsible	It's possible.
4. electrification	I need a vacation.
5. scientific	I'm terrific!
6. photography	It's hard for me!
7. economic	It's atomic.
8. institution	End pollution.
9. pronunciation	Let's tell the nation.

G
Check your progress: dialogue

Answers
X: What are you studying?
Y: Economics. What about you?
X: Photography.
Y: Then you must take good photographs.
X: And YOU must be good with money!

10 Word stress patterns

A

Stress patterns 🔊

Answers

hamburger	extremely	refrigerate
cookies	accurate	refrigerator
pizza	machine	refrigeration

One way to help students notice stress placement is to read a dialogue that the students can see in print, stressing the wrong syllable in some of the words. Can the class identify the wrong stresses?

B

Two-syllable names and phrases

Ask students to help you make a list of well-known names (singers, actors, presidents, etc.) with two syllable names, either first or last. You could also use the familiar names of people in the school or work environment where you teach. Most two-syllable names will fit into this basic stress pattern, although some foreign-influenced names will not, such as Marilyn Mon**roe**.

Note:

President Lincoln = U.S. president, 1861–1865
Prime Minister Macdonald = Canadian prime minister; 1867–1873 and 1878–1891
Charlie Chaplin = Actor and movie producer (1889–1977)
Jodie Foster = Movie actress and director
Judy Garland = Movie actress and singer (1922–1969)
Michael Jackson = Pop singer
Peter Jennings = TV news anchor

Dolly Parton = Country and western singer and movie actress
Elvis Presley = Rock singer and movie actor (1935-1977)
Robert Redford = Movie actor and director

J

Combined words

There is a stress difference between an adjective followed by a noun and a compound noun, as indicated by the following pairs:

Adjective + noun	Compound noun
black bird	blackbird (a particular kind of bird)
white house	White House (the home of the U.S. president)
green house	greenhouse (a special building for growing plants)
hard disk	hard disk (the fixed storage disk in a computer)

An example of this difference is the pair "lighthouse keeper/light housekeeper." "Light housekeeping" means a job which does not include heavy cleaning, but Edna Ferber had this to say of her housemaid, who was a lighthouse keeper's daughter: "Housekeeping in a lighthouse must be light housekeeping indeed, for the housemaid's ideas on the subject were airy to the point of nonexistence" (*A Peculiar Treasure*, 1940, p. 332).

Prator and Robinett (1985: 21) give some rough rules for the stress pattern of compounds.

1. Compound *nouns* generally have the stress on the first part (drugstore, thoroughfare, weatherman).

2. Compound *verbs* generally have the stress on the second part (understand, overlook, outrun).

These rules fit well with the stress patterns for two-word verbs in Exercise I of this unit. There seems to be a general "verbness" about stressing the second part.

Note: All of these patterns can be overridden by the needs of sentence emphasis. That is because the English speaker uses sentence accents to make the most important words more noticeable. If these accents are too close together, they tend to detract from each other's importance. For that reason, English speakers have a tendency to separate these accents by shifting the normal stress.

For example:

There are thir**teen** of them.
Thirteen **men** and **thir**teen **wo**men.

L

Check yourself

1st Commuter: What business are you in?
2nd Commuter: Photography.
1st Commuter: Oh yeah? Interesting. Is there a lot of money in it?
2nd Commuter: Well, ... look out... They can eat up your profit.
1st Commuter: Eat it up? ... set up a business like that?
2nd Commuter: The setup is expensive— chemicals, photographic ...
1st Commuter: ...I'll just stick to my present occupation.

11 Basic Emphasis Pattern: content words

Students will be more easily understood and will also hear English better if they learn to use the Basic Emphasis Pattern on which English speakers unconsciously rely.

Unit 10 further developed the effect of stress patterns on the rhythm of words. Unit 11 addresses the rhythm of a full sentence. Adult learners benefit from conscious attention to the features of rhythm in words (syllable length, stressed syllables, full and reduced vowels) and sentences (the effects of linking), and the way in which words are made prominent by extra lengthening of their stressed syllables (Wong 1987: 24).

This unit covers content words; Unit 12 covers structure words. The distinction between content word and structure word is a division found in all languages, but few people are consciously aware of these categories. You can help Japanese students recognize the difference between content words and structure words by mentioning the difference between the *kana* and the *kanji* characters in written Japanese. The kana (characters representing syllable sounds) are generally used to "spell" structure words; the kanji (characters representing whole ideas) are generally used to convey content words.

Demonstration Technique

A good way to illustrate emphasis is with a highlighter pen, which can be used to add color over words without obscuring the words. Highlighters are often used by students to mark important material for study because highlighting makes the marked words more noticeable. "Highlight" is more or less synonymous with "emphasize."

B
Locating content words

1. Do you like the picture on your passport?
2. Did you take a test for a driver's license in this country?
3. University students pay a lot of money for their books.
4. High school students get their books free.
5. Do you think it is harder to speak or to hear a new language?
6. Is there a speed limit for cars in your country?

G
Dialogue 📼

Answers

The content words are:

what	where
matter	put
lost	knew
glasses	find

H
Note taking 📼

Successful note taking generally consists of writing the content words and then guessing the structure words. This is an essential stage in achieving good listening comprehension.

Play the cassette or read the story on page 30 aloud or use another story if it would be more appropriate for your students.

This morning I waited and waited for the mail to come. I was expecting to get important news. Finally a letter came from the local school. It was a letter offering me a job as a teacher of the third grade! This will be my first teaching job, and I'm glad to get the opportunity to start my career.

Check yourself

2 Answers
Which "content" is a noun? The first "content."

Review

Linking: stop-to-stop

For Japanese students, the timing delay of "p" + "p" in "stop pushing" is similar to a phenomenon in Japanese words such as "Sapporo."

12 Basic Emphasis Pattern: structure words

Many English learners are suspicious of reductions, including contractions, because they regard them as substandard usage. This feeling can produce a covert resistance during exercises on these aspects of pronunciation. It may be helpful for you to emphasize that although contractions are not customary in formal *written* English, they are a necessary part of *spoken* English.

Reduction is a systematic way to downplay the less important words in order to more fully highlight the important ones. This contrast between highlighted and reduced words is fundamental to communication in English. In Unit 14 the students will find that giving the full form of structure words has specific meanings that they may not intend.

F
Reduced can 🔲

The distinction between "can" and "can't" has been reintroduced at a number of points in this course: as an example of the stop/continuant distinction, as a practice for linking, as an example of the difference between reduced and full vowels, and now from the standpoint of sentence emphasis. The purpose of this "spiraling" of the same pair of words is to demonstrate to the students how different parts of pronunciation are systematically interrelated.

In Unit 14, "Focus 2: emphasizing structure words," students will learn that it matters whether or not "can" is emphasized. Because this emphasis is so important for signaling the intent of the speaker, there must be a redundancy of signals. If "can" is to be emphasized, then the signals of lengthening, pitch change, and vowel clarity all

work together to bring the word to the listener's attention.

I
Pair practice: linking over the H

Demonstration techniques

1. *Folded Sentences* (this is another use of the technique provided on page 9). On a long piece of paper, put sentences using **H** pronouns, such as "Tell him something" or "Read her book." Make a pleat in the paper so that the space after the first word and the "h" of the next word are eliminated when you fold the pleat. Show your students the full sentence. Then fold the pleat so that the first two words look like one: "Tellim" or "Reader." This is an easy way to demonstrate the difference between printed English and spoken English.

2. *Vanishing Letters.* This is a further use of the red screen technique presented on page 4. If the class is in a low mood (middle of the semester, too much rain, etc.), this activity can provide a change of pace and subject. Give each student a piece of clear red plastic (a report cover can be cut into 8 pieces) and a yellow pencil or crayon. Ask students to write the dialogue for "The Missing Singer" (or compose a new dialogue with "he," "him," "his," or "her") on a piece of white paper, using the yellow pencil to write all silent "h" letters. The yellow pencil must be pressed very lightly for this activity to work. Demonstrate with chalk on the board. If you don't have yellow chalk, just print the "h" extra lightly. When students place the red plastic "screen" over their writing, the light yellow letters will vanish and the screened page will provide a read-aloud script

with blank spaces to remind them of the existence of the silent "h" letters. This technique uses both the concentration required to stop and change pencils and the visual image of the blank space to focus attention on the point being learned. The physical effort of changing pencils and writing lightly is added to mental recognition. Collect the equipment after use.

You can also use the "Vanishing Letters" equipment for a more competitive activity. Divide the class into teams, or have each student race against time. Write a few words with silent letters on the board (island, knife, walk). Give students five minutes to think of as many words with silent letters as possible. At the end of five minutes, a reporter from each group can write their list on the board, or the students can dictate their lists to you. Because people generally think of these words in patterns (light, right, night, etc.) students' lists will organize the words into sets for good practice. Have everybody copy the whole list, switching pencils for the silent letters. Then, with the red screen over the list, students can take turns reading the words aloud. If a student has not remained alert while writing the list, the filtered script will not blank out the silent letters.

As you circulate among the teams during their five-minute group work, you can offer the following words to any team that seems stuck:

> could, would, should
> ought, bought, thought
> Wednesday
> hour, honest
> comb, bomb
> knife, knee, knock, know
> sign, muscle, subtle

J

Dictation ▭

If you read these sentences aloud instead of using the cassette, be careful not to sound the "h" in the pronouns.

Answers

1. Did he give her the book?
2. Can he read her writing?
3. Is this his own work?
4. Where did he go with her car?
5. Why would he give her the information?

L

Reduced **T**: present tense ▭

Play the cassette or read these sentences aloud.

Answers

1. We want to go on a trip.	Slow, full
2. I wanna buy a car.	Fast, reduced
3. They want to buy a present.	Slow, full
4. I think they're gonna leave.	Fast, reduced
5. Are you gonna show us your work?	Fast, reduced
6. What are you going to do now?	Slow, full
7. I want to study now.	Slow, full
8. Why d'you wanna work so hard?	Fast, reduced
9. Because I want to succeed.	Slow, full
10. Because you wanna be rich?	Fast, reduced

M

Reduced **T**: past tense ▭

Play the cassette or read these sentences aloud.

Answers

1. They wanna call home.	Present
2. We wandeda go.	Past
3. I wanna eat.	Present
4. The children wandeda play.	Past
5. The actors wandeda see the theater.	Past

Extended practice

If you or your students have access to English language newspapers, pass out advertisements from the newspaper and have the students circle the content words. In classified advertisements, structure words are left out for the sake of brevity. The same thing is true for newspaper headlines. Advice columns like "Dear Abby" can be used to show contractions since they are usually written in an informal style. Comic strips are another good source of practice because they often use respelling in order to convey actual speech. You can give students a comic strip and ask them to "decipher" such respellings as "woulda," "I've got 'em," and "lemme just say."

13 Focus 1: pitch patterns used for emphasis

The functions of intonation

Intonation is commonly thought of as having the following two functions:

1. Distinguishing sentence types, for instance, questions versus statements.

2. Showing the speaker's attitude: excitement, pleasure, annoyance, and so on.

Distinguishing between questions and statements is useful, but it does not go very far. The second concept, concerning the expression of *feelings*, seems useful, but in practical classroom terms, it is vague and subject to bewildering variation.

A more practical approach to teaching intonation is to concentrate on its *primary* functions (Daneš 1960):

1. Highlighting the focus of meaning.
2. Dividing speech into thought groups.

Emphasis on the focus word highlights the contrast between new information and old information. All languages have one or more ways to show this difference, but English relies on intonation for this purpose more than most other languages. For that reason, learning to hear this emphasis, although difficult, is important. Students typically miss spoken signals of contrast with something said or assumed previously. When they learn to notice this intonation signal and recognize the implications, students take a major step forward in listening comprehension. However, it is not enough to emphasize some words. It is equally necessary to *de-emphasize* so that there is a contrast (Allen 1971: 81).

The need for teaching pitch

Although there are various cues to sentence emphasis, such as extra lengthening of the stressed syllable in the focus words, the most important signal is a change in pitch (Bolinger 1986: 21).

People have a tendency to speak a new foreign language in a monotone. Perhaps this is because they are tense or are concentrating on vocabulary and grammar. This is especially damaging for learners of English because pitch changes (melody) are such an essential part of the way English conveys which words are more important than others. Therefore, helping students to become aware of this use of melody may be one of the most effective and important contributions we can make to clarifying their speech.

Emphasis on a focus word is signaled by calling attention to the stressed syllable of that word in three ways: vowel lengthening, pitch change, and vowel clarity. A native speaker uses all three signals, but the student may do better concentrating just on lengthening and pitch change as the most easily controlled. If there has been adequate practice of lengthening in previous course work, adding pitch should be a manageable task at this point.

Demonstration technique: using a kazoo

The kazoo is an excellent tool for making the teaching points of this unit vivid. A kazoo is a toy instrument into which you *hum* a melody. The kazoo amplifies the voicing sound made by the vibration of the vocal cords. This technique of conveying speech eliminates all the distractions of grammar, vocabulary, and individual sounds so that students can concentrate on melody. Inexpensive plastic kazoos are generally available at toy stores or party goods shops. If you can get a large supply at a low price, it is helpful to give these to the students to use themselves. Students are always amused when they first see these toys but soon come to realize that they are serious tools for learning.

D

Pair practice: dialogues 🔊

2 Dialogues 1, 2, and 3 are almost exactly the same pattern.

1. X: Where are you <u>going</u>? (final content word)

   Y: <u>Europe</u>.

   X: Where in <u>Europe</u>?

   To the <u>north</u> or to the <u>south</u>? (equal options)

   Y: <u>Neither</u>. I've seen the <u>north</u> and the <u>south</u>.

   I'm going <u>east</u>.

2. X: What are they <u>building</u>?
   Y: They're building a <u>school</u>.
   X: What <u>kind</u> of school?
   <u>Elementary</u> or <u>high</u> school?
   Y: <u>Neither</u>. I think it's a <u>trade</u> school.

Dialogue 3, "Two Students," has the variation of a possible emphasis in the last line on either "always" or "hungry" or both if the speaker is excited. Dialogue 4, "A Tourist," offers somewhat more choice. Students can benefit from discussion, either in small groups or as a class, of the meaning of different choices of emphasis.

F

Pair practice: dialogue 🔊

In Speaker A's remark "Extra ones that they don't need," either "extra" or "need" could be emphasized. Or both could be emphasized because these are basically two separate thought groups. See

Unit 16, page 108 of the Student's Book, for a definition of thought groups. Each thought group has a focus word.

G

Pair practice: guessing what comes next

This exercise is an introduction to *prediction*, which is a critical skill in effective language use, both in conversation and for reading comprehension. Prediction ("guessing forward") helps the listener keep on track. If the next remark does not match the prediction, this is a warning that the conversation has gone off track and must be repaired immediately. That is, the listener must either make a rapid reassessment of what the speaker is talking about or *ask*. Without this warning of error, the conversation can continue for some time in the wrong direction.

Demonstration technique

This pair activity can be done very well using the kazoo. First use the kazoo to hum one of the choices and then ask students whether they heard choice (a) or (b). As a further challenge, use the kazoo to hum one of the choices, and ask students to give the correct response just as if they had heard the words. After this introduction, the class can follow the same procedure for pair practice. Student 1 hums (or uses a kazoo for) the remark and Student 2 answers accordingly. A kazoo works better than humming because it is easier to hear in a noisy classroom.

H

Disagreement

Students need not only to learn ways of showing disagreement, but also to recognize the signals when someone else is disagreeing with *them*.

Extended practice

"Pizza restaurant" (provided by Joseph Nicholson). Have students make a menu for a pizza restaurant by listing all the pizza toppings they can think of (cheese, onions, salami, pepperoni, pineapple, tomato, anchovies, etc.). Have them count the syllables for each topping, and underline the stressed syllable.

Then have the students write a dialogue for a Clerk and Customer. Students should write the dialogue so that there are confusions in the order that must be corrected. This gives an opportunity to use contrastive emphasis. Questions the Clerk might ask include:

Would you like mozzarella or parmesan cheese on your pizza?

What kind of topping do you want?

Do you want to eat it here or take it home?

Would you like a medium, large, or extra large size?

Example

Customer: I thought you said the medium was 14 inches. It looks small to me.

Clerk: I'm sorry, but I said the *large* was 14 inches. The medium is only *12* inches.

What was said?

Native speakers of any language rapidly pick up clues about the topic of discussion by the vocabulary and the emphasis used. This helps them get quickly oriented in the conversation even if they did not clearly hear what was said before. This "guessing backward" is a great help in listening comprehension. Both guessing forward and guessing backward, based on intonational emphasis, are further developed in Unit 14.

14 Focus 2: emphasizing structure words

There are two simultaneous teaching points in this lesson. First, the concept of focus words is extended into more complicated language use. It is extremely difficult but essential for students to begin to think of words not simply as they relate to sentences but also as they relate to the whole discourse structure.

Second, recognizing implications and predicting future developments are as essential to listening comprehension as they are to reading comprehension. In reading, vocabulary and context give important clues; in speaking, however, intonational emphasis is added to aid the listener, who is unable to read back over the material. For instance, an English listener recognizes the possible significance of the remark, "The lion *was* hungry." Without special emphasis for the "to be" verb, the sentence is a simple statement. But *with* the emphasis, the sentence implies a change of condition from the past.

C
Pair practice: **not**

It can be helpful to discuss Speaker B's attitude when saying "not." Speaker B might be angry, definite, argumentative, or strongly opinionated. Students need to realize that apparent emphasis on words that are usually contracted may convey a message they do not intend.

I
Pair practice: what will come next?

This is an extension of earlier prediction exercises, but it requires the students to use their own words. This is one step closer to the demands of real speech, in which the speaker must not only compose the language but also keep track of the intonational emphasis simultaneously.

J
Pair practice: checking information

Students who have difficulty with listening comprehension are helped by learning skills for checking what they have not clearly understood or for asking for further clarification.

Different answers are possible for item 4, for example, "What time?" or "*When* is she coming?"

K
Pair practice: what was said?

This exercise provides further practice in guessing backward in order to get oriented in a conversation.

O
Pair work: writing a dialogue

Give students suggestions to help them get started or ask them to develop topics in a group first. For example:

Detective movies are more entertaining than cowboy movies.
Hearing a new language is more difficult than speaking it.
The heaviest meal of the day should be lunch.

It is generally best to avoid topics that may cause real friction because heated emotion detracts from paying attention to the point of the lesson.

Extended practice: "Birds of a Feather"

This game (provided by Elpida Sklavos) is based on the saying, "Birds of a feather flock together." It gives students an opportunity to review syllable number, vowel length, and sentence emphasis by becoming kazoo-playing birds. At the end of the game, students should all be sorted into groups with the same "bird song" (intonation pattern).

Materials: Each student needs a copy of the list of "bird sentences" (below), a strip of paper containing one of the bird sentences, and a kazoo. If kazoos are not available, the intonation pattern can be hummed or sung with an "ahhh" vowel.

"Bird sentences"

1. Blue Bird: "I have beautiful blue feathers."
2. Rooster: "I can wake you up in the morning."
3. Parrot: "I can talk like a person."
4. Hummingbird: "I'm a very little bird."

Procedure

1. Give students copies of the bird sentences list. They should work in pairs to count the syllables in each sentence, mark the reduced vowels, and underline the emphasized syllables. The partners can then practice reading each sentence aloud while you circulate to check their marking.

2. Hand out kazoos and lead a kazoo band (or "ahhh" singing chorus) in a rehearsal of the rhythm and melody of each sentence.

3. Give a bird sentence strip to each student (students must not show their sentence to anybody else). The students then individually practice the melody of their sentences on the kazoo, memorizing the pattern so that it can be played (or sung) without looking at the strip.

4. Have students circulate and play their sentence to each other, looking for members of their "flock."

5. As students find members of their flock, have them stand together until all the birds in the flock have been gathered. The first complete flock wins. When all the teams are formed, "flocks" may take turns playing their tunes while the rest of the class decides which bird they are, referring to their copies of "bird sentences."

Variation of plan for small classes: Have only two strips of each bird sentence for the class. Students may then find their partner by matching the tune.

Intonation: pitch direction of questions

Different languages use pitch direction to mean different things. This source of confusion is seldom recognized when a conversation goes wrong. Following are two real-life samples (provided by Tom Scovel) of Thai versus English.

1. In the United States: An American bank manager and a Thai employee.

Manager: Where is Mr. Somsak?

Employee: He is si'.

Manager: (*unable to identify the final Thai stop sound*)

What?

Thai: (*unsure about what went wrong, decides it was the final **K** and also the falling tone; he therefore corrects himself as best he can*)

He is sick.

Manager: (*thinks "Why is he asking me?" and decides to avoid this employee in the future*)

2. In Thailand: A Thai language teacher and an American student of Thai.

Teacher: (*rising tone, rising tone, low tone*)

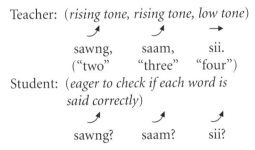

sawng, saam, sii.
("two" "three" "four")

Student: (*eager to check if each word is said correctly*)

sawng? saam? sii?

Teacher: (*thinks "How come they can learn to say "two" and "three," but when they get to "four," they always say "color"?*)

Aside from different uses of pitch patterns in different languages, the foreign language learner's tendency to speak in a monotone means that directing attention to final pitch direction can make a considerable difference in understandability.

Another way to look at pitch direction at the end of sentences is in relation to *sureness* and *unsureness*. A rising intonation at the end of a sentence often means the speaker is uncertain about something. On the other hand, a falling intonation at the end gives the impression of certainty. For this reason, a final rise is growing increasingly common in North America in the speech of people who wish to express the opposite of assertiveness. That is, it is instinctively felt to be friendlier not to end with a fall. Students need to understand this underlying message, as it could have significance in such situations as a job interview or a business conference. In certain situations, it might be better not to sound too assertive, whereas in other situations, it might be better not to sound uncertain.

Questions that ask for information with a question word

"Where are you going?" in number 1 reintroduces an intonation pattern students practiced in Unit 13 in the dialogue "A Traveler." All of these intonation patterns are "spiraled" in order to give review practice and also to provide deeper understanding of *why* the pattern is used.

C

Ways of checking information 📼

It is important for students to learn how to check information when they are not sure they heard something clearly. It is also helpful for them to recognize indications of uncertainty on the part of the person who is speaking to them. This is especially true in a work situation or any other circumstance where instructions or directions are being given.

Practice with checking information can be expanded by following with some natural challenges, such as these remarks, which contain a muffled (incomprehensible) part:

1. Where did mmmmmmm go?
2. We have to catch the bus at mmmmmm.
3. I'd like more mmmmmmmm, please.
4. Does anybody know where I left the mmmmmmm?

Wait after each remark. Students will be puzzled. After a suitable pause, ask them to answer you. Their first instinct will probably be to ask "What did you say?" or "Would you please repeat that?" You can then point out the advantage of not asking a general question ("What?") but a question that focuses specifically on the piece of information they need, such as "Who?" or "Where did *who* go?" This is like shining a flashlight beam on the exact information desired.

16 Intonation: thought groups (1)

Listeners get the impression of smooth continuity when someone is talking. In fact, most speech is a sequence of brief stops and starts. These short sequences are based on the speaker's effort to organize thoughts around separate ideas. It helps the listener if the words around each idea are clearly grouped.

The demarcation of thought groups is part of clear speech because it is an aid to comprehension. Students need to be taught about thought group markers because languages differ both in the way thought groups are marked and in the concept of what should be included in the group. For instance, Indo-European languages use pauses to mark groups, but many languages (Cantonese, Korean, and others) use clause-final particles (affixes), so they do not need to rely on intonation or timing to indicate group boundaries. Many languages (French, Spanish, Japanese, Turkish, and others), although they use pauses for this purpose, put boundaries in different places (Ballmer 1980).

Because of these differences, students may not even notice pauses. In fact, pauses are nearly as important as the correct stress pattern of a word or correct emphasis on sentence focus. For instance, if there are no pauses in the customary places, the English listener may have difficulty understanding (mentally recording) a series of numbers, no matter how clearly each number is pronounced. In general, the "chunking" of language is a necessary mechanism to aid listener processing.

Differences in intonational marking can cause a great deal of bad feeling between people because they are not aware of the reason for the difficulty. For instance, some East Indian languages use pitch fall as a signal that the speaker is about to make the most important point. Since the English listener will interpret the drop to mean "end of remark" or "I am finished speaking," there is apt to be serious misunderstanding. Unfortunately, people commonly mistake the intonation patterns of foreigners for insolence, indifference, or bad attitudes in general. Similarly, the politeness rules of one culture are often wrongly judged by people from another culture. For this reason, anyone wanting to do business of any kind in a foreign country will find practical advantage in learning some of the local rules.

In English, thought group boundaries are marked by three basic signals:

1. Pause
2. Pitch drop
3. Lengthening of final syllable

Examples: CNN, BBC, paper and pen

Thought grouping depends not only on a pitch fall but also on lengthening the final syllable. This phenomenon is demonstrated by the confusion in the following actual case: A Chinese-speaking student spent a long time looking for the apartment of his English-speaking friend, but finally gave up. The next day the two friends met in the university cafeteria.

American: I thought you were coming over yesterday.
Chinese: Yes, but no floor eight.
American: What?
Chinese: I looked for apartment 8237, but no floor eight.
American: Eight? But I live on floor *two*. Apartment A 237.
Chinese: Yes, yes. Apartment 8237.

American: No, that's not it. Apartment A 237.
Chinese: (silence)

Neither speaker realized that the American used lengthening of the "A," plus a pitch fall to separate A from the numbers that follow. Furthermore, the "A" was linked to the "two," making "A" sound like "eight" to the Chinese speaker, who would have sharply separated the A from the 2. Luckily, it occurred to them to write the apartment number on a piece of paper, but neither one had any idea why there was a problem.

A

Pair practice: telephone numbers

Other numbers can be used for this exercise, but the patterns of spacing may not be as simple. For instance, house addresses can be spoken in a number of ways; Social Security numbers, credit card numbers, and bank card numbers probably should not be dictated out loud; and passport numbers usually are not spaced. However, it is genuinely useful to practice the spacing of telephone numbers because it is a common problem for foreign travelers to have the listener (a telephone operator or some other person on the phone) misunderstand numbers given with a faulty grouping. Different countries have different spacing. For homework, you might suggest that students call Directory Assistance and ask for the telephone number of a business. (*Note:* Students may be charged for this call.) If the answer is given by a machine, it is made by a computer putting the individual numbers together in a string so that only the final one in each group will have a falling pitch.

C

Pair practice: arithmetic

Extended practice

If your students are used to dealing with algebraic equations, they will find it interesting and useful to practice reading them aloud. This can be done by having a student dictate equations to other students writing at the board. The equations can begin with a simple "$(A + B) \times C = Y$" and become as complex as suit the class. If the "thought groups" (i.e., items that are grouped by parentheses) are correctly indicated, the equations on the board should be correctly written. This is another case where instant and highly practical feedback can aid learning.

D

Either/or questions 🔲

This exercise is a reintroduction of the pattern already practiced in the first few dialogues in Unit 13.

Intonation: thought groups (2)

Small group work

Extended practice

An interesting way to demonstrate how North Americans and most Europeans show courteous interest is through a videotape with the sound turned off. Without the sound, it is easy to point out the frequent nods of the head, raised eyebrows, smiles, thoughtful frowns, and so on as the listener gives almost continuous physical feedback to reassure the speaker that he or she is being listened to attentively. Asian students in particular will find this enlightening because in most Asian cultures, courtesy requires not only silence when the other person is speaking but also a quiet manner. Although most Asians do nod or make little noises to show interest, the amount of such signaling is less than is typical for English speakers. This relative stillness of face is apt to be read by English speakers as enigmatic or even hostile. On the other hand, students from Latin or Middle Eastern cultures may benefit from the same silent video if you point out to them how far apart the people are when they talk to each other.

Summary of intonational signals

The concept of "road signs for the listener" is fundamental to communication. When students speak in class, they are typically thinking about avoiding mistakes in grammar, spelling, vocabulary, and so on. The one thing they are usually *not* thinking about is the listener. English listeners depend on intonational guides to help them follow the intentions of the speaker. English language learners typically do not use the English signals of intonational emphasis or thought grouping. Emphasis that conveys the wrong meaning or thought groups that are run together, or break in inappropriate places, cause extra work for the listener who is trying to follow the speaker's meaning. If the burden is too great, the listener simply stops listening.

The principle "help the listener to follow" is so central to communication that time spent helping students concentrate on *rhythm* and the *major intonational road signs* is more important than any other efforts to improve their pronunciation.

The great English novelist, E. M. Forster, expressed it this way:

A pause in the wrong place, an intonation misunderstood, and a whole conversation went awry.

(from *A Passage to India*)

Appendix A
Vowels

There is some research evidence to suggest that vowels, unlike consonants, are best learned initially through listening perception drills rather than speaking practice (Fucci, et al. 1977). That is why most of the vowel exercises here concentrate mainly on auditory perception practice.

Because vowels improve only very gradually, the most practical approach is to have modest expectations. If you hope for good English vowels by the end of the course, the result is apt to be discouraging. Perhaps the most we can do (and it is really quite a lot) is to teach students how to listen for these vowels, sorting them into English categories. As the learner gains better control of English rhythm, the vowels can gradually be shaped closer to the English target sounds.

C
Listening for vowel 11 ▭

If you are not using the cassette, be careful to say all the words in these sets with exactly the same intonation, so that you don't give away which is the "different" word. (The underlined word is different.)

Answers

1.	seem	sum	seem	(B)
2.	bake	bake	buck	(C)
3.	love	leave	leave	(A)
4.	ran	ran	run	(C)
5.	cap	cup	cap	(B)
6.	him	him	hum	(C)
7.	bed	bed	bud	(C)
8.	rain	rain	run	(C)
9.	bit	but	bit	(B)
10.	seem	seem	sum	(C)

D
Listening for vowels 1 and 2 (**he** and **him**) ▭

Play the cassette or read these words aloud. (The underlined word is different.)

Answers

1.	feel	feel	fill	(C)
2.	read	rid	read	(B)
3.	teen	teen	tin	(C)
4.	live	leave	leave	(A)
5.	he's	he's	his	(C)
6.	peel	peel	pill	(C)
7.	rich	reach	reach	(A)
8.	cheap	chip	cheap	(B)
9.	seen	seen	sin	(C)
10.	feet	fit	fit	(A)

H
Pair practice: dialogue ▭

Answers

       2 1 2 1 1   1   1
Sister: Billy, Billy, teach me to read!

              2
Brother: You're too little.

                    2   1 2
Sister: No, I'm not. I'm big. Very big!

        2 1   2   1
Brother: I'm busy. Here's a nickel for some candy.

        2   2   1 2 1
Sister: A nickel? That's too little! I need fifty
        cents.

              2   1 1   1
Brother: Hmmm. It would be cheaper to teach
          1
        you to read!

I

Review of vowel 11 (love) 🔊

Play the cassette or read these words aloud. (The underlined word is different.)

Answers

1. cat	cat	cut	(C)
2. fan	fun	fan	(B)
3. hat	hut	hat	(B)
4. done	done	dawn	(C)
5. some	some	same	(C)
6. rain	run	run	(A)
7. love	leave	leave	(A)
8. tab	tab	tub	(C)

K

Listening for vowels 3 and 8 (came and home) 🔊

Play the cassette or read these words aloud. (The underlined word is different.)

Answers

1. make	make	mike	(C)
2. bite	bat	bite	(B)
3. try	tray	try	(B)
4. fun	fun	phone	(C)
5. ban	bone	bone	(A)
6. say	say	so	(C)

Appendix B
Additional work on consonants

Demonstration techniques

If students have difficulty saying **R** or **L** and have been reading English for some time, they have developed a habitually wrong reaction to seeing the *letters* "r" and "l." Suggest to these students that they think of the letter "r" as short and bunched up, like the tongue drawn back for the **R** sound. The **L** sound is made with a long tongue, reaching to touch the tooth ridge, and shaped rather like the letter "l" in print.

Here's a more elaborate approach to breaking the "misreading" habit. Present students with a poster on which you have written words containing the difficult letters. Each problem letter should be replaced by a spot of color instead of the letter. Color coding can be made memorable by using yellow for "l" (as in the key word, "yellow") and red for "r" (as in "red"). It may help to make the yellow spot a tall rectangle (roughly the shape of "l") and the red spot a short square (roughly the shape of "r"). Prepare a "reading script" on a poster in this manner. After students have read the script aloud, have them read aloud from the same script with actual letters, but backed with the color code. Then ask them to reread the script aloud, but this time with all black letters.

Appendix C
Student's own dictation

If the relationship between speaker and listener is like an electrical circuit, then this exercise can be thought of as a "circuit failure analysis." It is a time-consuming activity, but it can be extraordinarily rewarding.

A
Dictation

The exercise works this way: Students are asked to bring to class one or two long sentences from their work or field of study. You may not be able to complete more than a few dictations at each class session, but the students can save their sentences until you get to them. Tell the class that they are going to dictate these sentences but that this is not going to be a listening test for the class. Students will be writing what they hear dictated in order to help the speaker analyze his or her own speech weaknesses. This can be useful for everybody because most errors are typical, and the students should be using the exercise to learn to avoid making the same mistakes. Group help for another student can build rapport in a class if it is not allowed to become group criticism.

Before starting the dictation, the speaker writes any unusual terms, especially technical jargon, on the board. After this preparation, the speaker reads the sentences aloud so that the class can hear the whole piece. Now the speaker dictates the sentences in phrases. If possible, this should be recorded. Students write what they hear, leaving blank spaces for words they cannot catch. Finally, the speaker reads the sentences again so that students can check their work.

Ask the speaker and two or three students to write their versions on the board. The listeners' versions can then be compared with the original.

Caution 1: This exercise is likely to be more successful in a mixed-language class. If students all speak the same language, they understand each other's English because their errors are all the same.

Caution 2: Students sometimes express doubts about the value of taking dictation from a nonnative speaker. The teacher can reassure the class that the exercise is valuable for both the speaker and the listener because it is often possible to distinguish between listener errors and speaker errors.

Caution 3: No matter how enthusiastic students are about the usefulness of this exercise, it rarely works as well with a "second round," when the students give dictations of new material.

B

Analysis

Take the student dictation yourself while the students are writing. Note all the errors you can. In particular, errors in emphasis and thought grouping are not likely to be noticed by the class, so you will need to have a record of them.

Circle the content words. If a content word is missing or if there is a serious sound error in it, the confusion is apt to extend for several words following because the listener is still trying to identify the first word. Also, the content word error may cause a mistaken idea later as the listener tries to make sense of the sentence. For instance, if a noun is thought to be a verb (or vice versa), there is bound to be confusion later in the sentence.

Syllables are frequently dropped, either in unstressed prefixes or (more commonly) in final syllables. Lack of a final "s" is the most common error, although many language groups lack any final consonant.

Individual sound errors often fall into the categories of the stop/continuant or the voiced/unvoiced contrast. This provides you with the opportunity for reviewing these differences.

It is not always easy to tell if the error was a speaking mistake or a listening mistake unless students from several language backgrounds hear it the same way. This is the advantage of having a recording of the dictation.

If you are a native speaker of English and an experienced teacher of the language, your ear will have a tendency to correct for errors automatically, so you may not notice them. However, even if you did not note the error yourself, you can probably assume that the speaker made a mistake if several class members (from different language groups) wrote the same thing.

If there was an unfamiliar idiom or technical word, students are apt to miss it and maybe also get confused for several words following. This is a good time to point out the importance of pronouncing an unusual term with special care.

Analysis of these dictations can provide a practical summary of everything you have taught the students in this course. After this analysis, and some class practice of the sentence, it is helpful to have the student record the dictation again for comparison with the first version.

Appendix D
Lecture: public speaking

Play the cassette or read this lecture aloud. Ask students to write a list of the main points and then compare their list with another student's list. Did both students notice the same points?

Note: The following lecture does not appear in the Student's Book.

Evaluation of listening comprehension

There are various methods for evaluating the students' understanding of this lecture. They could be asked simply to take notes and compare them with a partner. A small group discussion could yield a consensus of rules for good presentations, which could then be dictated to a group member at the board. This set of rules can then be incorporated into a "judging sheet," which can be used later for evaluating other students' presentations (in Appendix E on pages 49–50).

 Public Speaking

In university work or in business situations, you may be expected to give oral reports. It's important to keep in mind that written reports and spoken reports are quite different. If you want to be clearly understood, you can't simply read a written report out loud. There are several things you can do to make your oral reports clear and easy to understand.

The first rule of public speaking is to strictly limit the amount of information you want to present. Decide what main points are absolutely necessary, and then limit your talk to these points. The biggest difference between spoken and written language is that readers can look back over printed words when they don't understand. With *spoken* language, however, listeners can't go back and check the words. They have to rely on memory. This means that an oral report can't deliver as much information as a written report. That is, you can't have as many pieces of information packed into the same number of words.

The second rule of public speaking is to deliver the information slowly enough so that listeners can recognize each main point. One good way to help your audience is simply to speak slowly. Many people speak too fast when they address an audience. This is a mistake because rapid speech makes listening more difficult. Beyond the simple technique of speaking more slowly, the best way to help listeners follow your ideas is to pause after each main point. Even if you speak quickly in between pauses, each pause gives your listeners time to think about what you have just said. Listeners need to fit these ideas into their own knowledge of the subject. Besides pausing, you can slow down the rate of information by saying the same thing in different words. This helps listeners to process each idea before the next idea is explained.

The third rule of public speaking is to make sure your listeners recognize your main points. Use intonation to emphasize the focus words in each main point. It's not so important that listeners hear all the words clearly, but it's *very* important that the focus words are clearly recognized.

There's an added advantage to taking the time to think about how to make your oral report more understandable. Simplifying the main points, marking places for pauses, and underlining the main focus words are all techniques that can help you to prepare a simple outline. Speaking from this outline will make a much better speech than reading from a script.

In summary, a good public speaker limits the main points, gives listeners time to think after each main point, and emphasizes the focus words.

Appendix E
Students' oral reports

Ask the students to prepare a five-minute talk on their field of work or some other topic. This talk must not be read from a script, but delivered from outline notes. Be strict about the time allowance. It promotes more careful planning if the speaker knows the time is limited.

While a student is giving a talk, the rest of the class should take notes. (If possible, the talk should be recorded for study at home or in the language laboratory.)

Judging by the ease with which they could take notes from the talk, the class should help the speaker analyze the clarity of the oral report. The following points should be considered:

1. *Amount of information.* Was there too much for a five-minute talk?

2. *Focus Words.* Were focus words clearly pronounced?

3. *Technical terms (or especially important new information).* Were there adequate pauses after unfamiliar technical terms and new information, to allow the listener time to think about what was just said?

4. *Organization.* Was the talk in logical sequence to help the listener predict what might come next?

5. *Did the speaker make it easy for the listener to follow?* That is the essence of clear speech.

If your class has developed a list of rules for judging oral presentations, as suggested on page 48 in Appendix D, this can be used for analyzing the talk; that is, noting the careful emphasis of focus words, thought grouping, and other "navigational" aids for the listener. Many students will not have realized previously that they have an obligation to make their talks comprehensible as well as thorough.

Most teachers understand that language practice is more effective if there is a genuine communicative intent – that is, if the speaker is telling the listeners something they did not already know. This lesson should be a natural way to put that principle into action. Unfortunately, traditionally trained students quite frequently see this sort of exercise as simply another way for the speaker to practice correct English while the class, politely deaf, thinks about other things. Students may need help recognizing that they have a responsibility beyond correctness. As speakers, they have a

responsibility to make their reports easily understandable; as listeners, they have a responsibility to
make an effort to understand.

Testing

One way to overcome a reluctance to accept
mutual responsibility is to use a traditional tool:
testing. Ask each speaker to prepare three questions for a quiz on the talk. The class should take
notes during the talk to prepare for the quiz.

The questions can be read aloud after the talk.
If most of the class can answer the questions, then
the point was clearly conveyed. On the other
hand, if the class as a whole cannot answer (i.e.,
give the answer the speaker considers correct), you
can ask "How can this talk be improved so that
the audience would have been able to answer that
question?" One helpful suggestion is to restate the
main ideas in the conclusion of the talk. A surprising number of students are unaware of the effectiveness of a concluding summary.

A useful way to look at the "failed" questions is
that the point of the question may not have been
worth much attention. Students often write questions on details simply because they are easy to
write or because the student thinks the purpose of
a quiz question is to be difficult. It is important
for the class to realize that the main function of
this post-talk quiz is to test the true effectiveness
of the talk. Also, the students should begin to see
that the formulation of the questions is a way to
determine which main thoughts they really want
their talk to convey. Not only does this encourage
students to limit the amount of information in
their reports but it also gives them the beginning
of a strong structure, or outline. Clear structure is
the necessary basis for a clear talk and lends itself
well to the practice of the intonational signals that
help the listener to follow: pause and emphasis.

Appendix F
Lectures for listening practice

Following are three research report lectures. The first lecture is quite short, about the length of an average TOEFL listening comprehension lecture. The second and third are much longer.

Play the cassette or read the lectures aloud. Ask students to take notes as they listen. They should not try to write everything they hear, but concentrate on catching the focus words. After each lecture, ask students to reconstruct what was said from their notes, either in writing or orally. This could be a good small group task.

Lectures

A. "Age and Language Learning"

B. "Pronunciation Achievement Factors"

C. "Thought Group Markers"

A
Age and Language Learning* 🔲

Most people think that the older you get, the harder it is to learn a new language. That is, they believe that children learn more easily and efficiently than adults. Thus, at some point in life, maybe around age 12 or 13, people lose the ability to learn languages well. Is this idea fact or myth?

Is it true that children learn a foreign language more efficiently than adults? On the contrary, research studies suggest that the opposite may be true. One report on 2000 Danish children studying Swedish concluded that the teenagers learned more in less time than the younger children. Another report on Americans learning Russian showed a direct improvement of ability over the age range tested; that is, the ability to learn increased as the age increased from childhood to adulthood.

There are several possible explanations for these findings. For one thing, adults know more about the world and therefore are able to understand meanings more easily than children. Moreover, adults can use logical thinking to help themselves see patterns in the language. Finally, adults have more self-discipline than children.

All in all, it seems that the common idea that children are better language learners than adults may not be fact but myth.

---

* Adapted from E. Hatch, "Optimal age or optimal learners?" *Workpapers in Teaching English as a Second Language,* Vol. X (1977): 45–56, and from S. Krashen, M. Long, and R. Scarcella, "Age, rate, and eventual attainment in second language acquisition," *TESOL Quarterly,* Vol. 13 (1979): 573–582.

B

Pronunciation Achievement Factors *

We all know that it's difficult for adults to learn accurate pronunciation in a foreign language. We also know that some people achieve better results than others. Why is this? What are the factors that might predict which students will achieve good pronunciation? If we knew the factors helping pronunciation, we could improve our own learning.

Richard Suter, a language researcher at a California university, decided to test the relative importance of factors that might predict which students would achieve the most accurate pronunciation. He wanted to find out if there were any factors a student could change in order to improve performance.

The first thing Suter did was to make a list of all the factors that might possibly show which students would learn the best pronunciation. Then he compared these factors with the pronunciation of a group of nonnative speakers of English. Here is a list of six of the factors that Suter studied.

1. *Gender.* Do females learn better than males?

2. *Mother tongue.* Is it easier to learn a language close to one's own?

3. *Personality.* Do outgoing people learn pronunciation better than shy people?

4. *Attitude toward pronunciation.* Does it make a difference if the student believes that pronunciation is a very important part of language?

5. *Natural ability.* How important is the ability to mimic, or imitate? Most people assume that natural ability is the single most important factor in learning pronunciation.

6. *Conversation with native speakers.* Does the amount of conversation in English with native speakers of English make a significant difference?

When Suter compared the students' pronunciation accuracy scores with these six variables, he discovered some surprising results. He found that two of the factors were not at all significant in predicting who would do well learning pronunciation. These two factors were:

1. *Gender.* Females were not better learners than males.

2. *Personality.* Outgoing people were not better at pronunciation than shy people.

Suter concluded from these results that the factors of gender and personality were not significant predictors of pronunciation accuracy. On the other hand, he found

---

*Adapted from R. Suter, "Predictors of pronunciation accuracy in second language learning," *Language Learning,* Vol. 26, No. 2. (1976): 233–253.

that four variables did make a significant difference. I will give them to you in order of importance. That is, the most important predictors come first.

1. *Mother tongue.* This was the most significant factor in predicting achievement. If the student's own language was closer to English, the achievement was likely to be greater.

2. *Attitude about pronunciation.* This was the second most important factor in predicting achievement. In fact, a belief in the importance of pronunciation was far more important than any of the remaining factors. After the mother tongue factor, this factor of attitude was the single most significant variable in predicting good pronunciation learning.

3. *Conversation with native speakers.* The third most important variable was the amount of time the student spent in conversation with native speakers of English.

4. *Natural ability.* This was the least important variable. The ability to imitate helped, but it was not nearly as significant as most people think. It was far less significant than the first three.

Suter concluded that the three most significant predictors in achievement in pronunciation are (1) the student's mother tongue, (2) the belief in the importance of pronunciation, and (3) the amount of time spent in conversations with native speakers.

The conclusions of this research are encouraging. Of course, we can't change factor 1, our mother tongue. But we *do* have control over factors 2 and 3, which are the next most important variables in learning accurate pronunciation. First, we can decide that pronunciation is important, and second, we can choose to make the effort to speak the new language with native speakers. You might say that our own choice is the most significant factor in achievement in the new language.

C

Thought Group Markers * ▭

Today I want to tell you about some useful research on the way English speakers help their listeners. You know that a lot of English sentences are very complicated. The listener can get confused if the thought groups aren't clearly divided. If the groups aren't clear, the ideas won't be clear.

Each language has special ways to mark thought groups. In English the chief marker is intonation. A researcher named O'Malley thought of a clever way to study these markers. He knew that algebra problems have to be written with parentheses. These punctuation markers are used to group the terms. If the algebra is spoken out loud, a native speaker of English can hear the grouping. Let me give you an example. Write down this equation:

$$A + (B \times C) = Y$$

Now write down another one:

$$(A + B) \times C = Y$$

Did you write them differently? You should have put the parentheses in different places because these equations are different.

Perhaps you can get the idea better if I use examples from arithmetic. Write down this problem:

$$2 + (3 \times 4) = 14$$

Now write:

$$(2 + 3) \times 4 = 20$$

Did you put the parentheses in different places? The terms are exactly the same, but the grouping is different. That is why the answers are different.

The same concept of grouping also applies to words. Here's an example:

"John," said the boss, "is stupid."

That has a very different meaning from this sentence, using the same words:

John said, "The boss is stupid."

The meaning is different, just as in algebra or arithmetic. So grouping is important. Of course, speaking isn't like writing. We don't use parentheses or other punctuation when we're speaking. In fact, punctuation was invented to try to show some of the things we do in speech to separate groups of words. Written language substitutes punctuation for the spoken signals of intonation. The English listener depends on these intonation signals in order to understand clearly.

In his research on the subject of thought-group markers, O'Malley tape-recorded native English speakers reading algebraic equations aloud. Then he asked some other English speakers to listen to the recordings and decide where the parentheses were placed. O'Malley found that both the speakers and the listeners were very consistent in grouping the terms. The listeners were able to identify the placement of the parentheses because the speakers used three main markers to show the end of a group.

The first marker was *silence*. That is, the speaker paused after the group to make clear that it was finished. Listen for the pause when I read this equation:

$$A \ldots + (B \times C) \ldots = Y$$

Marker 1, a pause, is quite powerful in slow speech. But in more rapid speech, there

---

*Adapted from M. O'Malley, D. Kloker, and B. Dara-Abrams, "Recovering parentheses from spoken algebraic expressions," *IIEE Transactions on Audio and Electro-Acoustics,* AU-21 (1973): 217–220.

isn't time for many pauses. So the speaker has to rely on other signals to mark the end of a group. Marker 2 is a change of pitch. Usually the voice pitch drops low at the end of a group. Generally, a high pitch means a new idea and a low pitch means the end of an idea. Listen for the pitch change when I read this equation:

$$(A + B) \times C = Y$$

Marker 3 is a lengthening of the final syllable of the group. Listen to the equation once more, this time paying attention to the lengthening at the end of each group:

$$(A + \underline{B}) \times \underline{C} = \underline{Y}$$

Other researchers** have confirmed these findings for spoken English. In both algebraic formulas and spoken English, the thought groups are divided by the same three markers. With marker 1, which is especially used for slow speech, the speaker pauses at the end of each group. With marker 2, the voice falls at the end of a group. With marker 3, the final syllable in each group is lengthened. For special clarity, all three markers are used.

I've reviewed some of this research because it shows a very important way to help our listeners understand us easily. The research demonstrates the ways of making thought groups clear. Clear thought groups are part of clear speech.

**D. Klatt, "Vowel lengthening is syntactically determined in connected discourse," *Journal of Phonetics,* Vol. 3 (1975): 139, and I. Lehiste, "Isochrony reconsidered," *Journal of Phonetics,* Vol. 5, (1977): 253–263.

Clear listening test answer key

The Clear Listening Test appears on page viii of the Student's Book. (A blank copy of this test, which can be photocopied and distributed to students, appears on pages 74–77 of this Teacher's Resource Book.) You can either play the cassette or read the test aloud, using the answer key that follows. Beginning the course with a test makes it possible for both you and your students to see what needs improvement. Most people do not realize that they are having trouble with such things as syllable number, contractions, or identifying stress. If you give the test again later in the course, the students will have an objective measure of progress. Of course, you should not give the test again unless the students have actually been thoroughly exposed to the concepts in the course and given adequate time to practice them.

The aim of the test is to catch some errors, so it must not be too easy; on the other hand, it should not be so difficult as to be overwhelming. To adjust to the level of your students, read all the items in the test only once (except the dictation in Part 4 and the focus for meaning in Part 6) for advanced students, but twice for intermediate students.

When you score the test, be strict. The purpose is to alert your students to the need for improvement so that they will pay attention to the following lessons. Students must learn to be sensitive to which syllable gets the stress if they wish to speak clearly; it is a mistake, therefore, to allow vague answers on this test. For instance, if the student underlined the wrong syllable or included two or more syllables in underlining stress, take off a point.

Clear Listening Test 📼

How you hear English is closely connected with how you speak English.

Part 1

Sounds

[10 points]

The following pairs of sentences are exactly the same except for one word. You will hear either sentence (a) or (b). Circle the letter of the sentence you hear.

Example a. Do you want everything?
b. **Do you wash everything?**

Teacher: Play the cassette or read the sentences in bold type.

1. (a.) **They save old bottles.**
b. They saved old bottles.

2. a. She loves each child.
(b.) **She loved each child.**

3. (a.) **Was a bath all he wanted?**
b. Was a bat all he wanted?

4. (a.) **He always spills everything.**
b. He always spilled everything.

5. (a.) **Did she bring her card every day?**
b. Did she bring her car every day?

6. (a.) **Which cuff do you like?**
b. Which cup do you like?

7. a. They've already gone.
(b.) **They'd already gone.**

8. a. We can often see the mountains.
(b.) **We can't often see the mountains.**

9. (a.) **Who'll ask you?**
b. Who'd ask you?

10. (a.) **We watch all of it.**
b. We wash all of it.

Part 2

Syllable number

[10 points]

How many syllables do you hear? Write the number.

Examples a. ease   _1_
b. easy   _2_
c. easily   _3_

1. closet	2	6. opened	2	
2. sport	1	7. first	1	
3. clothes	1	8. caused	1	
4. simplify	3	9. committee	3	
5. frightened	2	10. arrangement	3	

Part 3

Word stress   [10 points]

Draw a line under the syllable with the most stress (the strongest syllable). Mark only one syllable for each word.

Examples   a. de<u>lay</u>
              b. <u>bro</u>ken
              c. edu<u>ca</u>tion

1. par<u>ti</u>cipating
2. <u>pho</u>tograph
3. pho<u>to</u>graphy
4. Ca<u>na</u>dian
5. ge<u>o</u>graphy

6. <u>Eu</u>rope
7. infor<u>ma</u>tion
8. e<u>co</u>nomy
9. eco<u>no</u>mic
10. po<u>li</u>tical

Part 4

Contractions, reductions   [20 points]

You will hear a sentence. It will be read twice. Write the missing words.

Example   You hear: Do you think she's in her room?

You write: Do you think _____*she's*_____ in her room?
            or
            Do you think _____*she is*_____ in her room?

Teacher: **Read the sentence in informal style, as written above the sentence. Accept either a contraction or a full form. Do not count off for spelling errors if you can recognize the words. Give 2 points for each correct sentence.**

1.   *"who'll"*
     Who will _____ you ask?

2.   *"izziz"*
     Is his _____ work good?

3. *"where'll"*
    Where will _____ you go?

4. Please *"give 'em"*
    give them (*or* him; *not* me) _____ the information.

5. *"I've done"*
    I have (*or* I've) done _____ everything.

6. *"izzy"*
    Is he busy now? _____

7. *"how long've you"*
    How long have you been here? _____

8. *"why didy"*
    Why did he come so late to the office? _____

9. *"what's she"*
    What has she done lately? _____

10. *"he duzzen wanna"*
    He does not (*or* doesn't) want to study this morning. _____

Part 5

Focus: identification   [10 points]

You will hear a dialogue with ten sentences. In each sentence underline the word with the most emphasis (the strongest word).

Example A: That's a **great** idea!

A: Do you think food in this country is <u>expensive</u>?

B: Not <u>really</u>.

A: I think <u>it's</u> expensive.

B: That's because you eat in <u>restaurants</u>.

A: Where do <u>you</u> eat?

B: At <u>home</u>.

A: Can you <u>cook</u>?

B: Well, actually I <u>can't</u> cook. I just eat cheese.

A: That's <u>awful</u>!

Part 6

Focus: meaning [20 points]

The following pairs of sentences are exactly the same, except a different word is stressed (stronger) in each sentence. You will hear sentence (a) or (b) twice. Circle the correct response.

Example a. They bought two bottles. Not three?
     b. **They bought two bottles.** ⟨Not cans?⟩

Teacher: Give students time to read these sentences first. **Then play the cassette or read the sentences in bold type.**

1. a. **We want to buy a lot of apples.** ⟨Not oranges?⟩
    b. We want to buy a lot of apples. How many?

2. a. I think that animal is a wolf. No, it's a fox.
    b. **I think that animal is a wolf.** ⟨Aren't you sure?⟩

3. a. Frank wanted to go early. When?
    b. **Frank wanted to go early.** ⟨Who?⟩

4. a. **Sally writes the reports.** ⟨No, she reviews them.⟩
    b. Sally writes the reports. No, Bob does.

5. a. **Does she speak French?** ⟨No, but he does.⟩
    b. Does she speak French? No, but she can read it.

Part 7

Thought groups [20 points]

You will hear sentence (a) or (b) twice. Answer the question that follows the sentence you hear.

Example a. John said, "My father is here."
     b. **"John," said my father, "is here."**
     Question Who was speaking? *my father*

Teacher: **Play the cassette or read the sentences in bold type.**

1. a. **He sold his houseboat and car.**
    b. He sold his house, boat, and car.
    Question How many things did he sell? *two*

2. a. She likes pineapples.
    b. **She likes pie and apples.**
    Question How many things does she like? *two*

3. a. Would you like some soup or salad?
   b. **Would you like some Super Salad?**
   Question How many things were you offered? ___one___

4. a. The president said, "That reporter is lying."
   b. **"The president," said that reporter, "is lying."**
   Question Who was speaking? ___that reporter___

5. a. Wooden matches are used to start fires.
   b. **Wood and matches are used to start fires.**
   Question How many kinds of things are used
            to start fires? ___two___

Clear Speaking Test

Record this dialogue. Speak in a conversational style, as naturally as possible.

Teacher: **Listen to the student's tape while looking at a copy of the dialogue. Circle each error that you hear and then fill out a pronunciation profile form for each student. A master form appears on page 78.**

On the following pages is an analysis form of some of the possible errors.

At the Travel Agent's Office 🔲

A: [1] Can I help you?

B: [2] Yes, I want to fly to Chicago on Wednesday the seventh and return on Friday the ninth.

A: [3] Of October?

B: [4] No, November. How much is the fare?

A: [5] Fares are cheaper if you stay over Saturday night.

B: [6] Thanks, but unfortunately I've already arranged some business here that Friday. So I'll just have to pay the extra cost.

A: [7] What time of day would you prefer? Morning or afternoon?

B: [8] Morning, because I have to be there by early evening. Is there a meal?

A: [9] Yes, they'll be serving breakfast; and you'll also see a movie.

B: [10] Which movie?

A: [11] In both directions they'll show a short feature on planned communities. [12] Going east, the major film is *City Slickers*. [13] I think it's a cowboy comedy. [14] The movie going west is *Big Joe*. [15] That's an adventure story about a boy who raises a wolf.

B: [16] Sounds good, but what's the fare?

A: [17] Eight hundred and fifty dollars round trip.

B: [18] That's more than I expected!

Clear speaking test analysis form

This is only a partial list of possible errors, listed by numbered sentence.

A
Number of syllables

[2] fly (1 syll), Wednesday (2 syll), Friday (2 syll)
[5] Saturday (3 syll)
[6] unfortunately (5 syll), arranged (no final "ed" syllable), business (2 syll)
[11] planned (no final "ed" syllable), communities (4 syll)
[12] City (not "sit"), Slickers (2 syll)
[15] story (not "estory" or "sitory"), raises (final "es" syllable)
[17] eight hundred and fifty dollars (8 syllables)

Additional errors of syllable number: _____

B
Sounds

[2] **y**es, **fl**y, **Chi**cago (SH), se**ven**th, **Fr**iday, nin**th**
[3] Octo**b**er
[4] No**v**ember
[5] fare**s**, **ch**eaper, o**v**er
[6] **th**anks, I'**ve**, al**r**eady, **arr**an**g**ed, **b**usiness, **j**ust
[7] **w**ould, p**r**efer, **m**orning, aftern**oo**n
[8] **b**e, **e**arly, e**v**ening
[9] they'**ll**, ser**v**ing, **y**ou'll, **s**ee
[10] whi**ch**
[11] bo**th**, **sh**ow, **sh**ort
[12] ma**j**or, Slicker**s**
[13] **th**ink
[14] **w**est, **B**ig, **J**oe
[15] **th**at's, ad**ven**tu**r**e (CH), rai**s**e**s** (voiced), **w**olf
[16] sound**s**, **g**ood, **f**are
[17] eigh**t**, fif**t**y, dollar**s**

Additional errors of sounds: _____

C

Linking

[1] can I

[2] Chicago on, seventh and, return on

[3] Of October?

[5] fares are, cheaper if, stay over

[6] I've already arranged

[7] time of, morning or afternoon

[8] because I, by early evening

[9] you'll also see a movie

[11] show a, feature on

[12] going east, film is

[13] think it's a

[14] west is

[15] That's an adventure, about a boy, raises a wolf

Additional errors of linking: _____

D

Reduced vowels (unstressed syllables)

[2] Chicago, seventh

[6] arranged

[9] breakfast

[11] directions

[13] comedy

[15] adventure, raises

[17] hundred, dollars

Additional errors of failure to reduce vowels: _____

E

Reduced words

[1] can I ...

[2] I want to fly to Chicago on Wednesday the seventh and return ...

[3] Of October?

[5] Fares are cheaper ...

[6] just have to pay the extra ...

[7] What time of day ... morning or afternoon?

[8] a meal?

[9] breakfast, and ...

[13] I think it's a ...

[15] that's an adventure ... a wolf

[16] what's the fare?

Additional errors of failure to reduce words: _____

F

Stressed syllables (stress patterns)

[2] Chi**ca**go, **sev**enth, **Wed**nesday, re**turn**, **Fri**day

[3] Oc**to**ber

[4] No**vem**ber

[5] **cheap**er, **Sat**urday

[6] un**for**tunately, **al**ready, ar**ranged**, **bus**iness, **ex**tra

[7] pre**fer**, **mor**ning, after**noon**

[8] be**cause**, **ear**ly, **eve**ning

[9] **break**fast, **al**so, **mo**vie

[11] di**rec**tions, **fea**ture, com**mun**ities,

[12] **ma**jor, **City**, **Slick**ers

[13] **cow**boy, **com**edy

[15] ad**ven**ture, **rais**es

[17] **hun**dred, **fif**ty, **doll**ars

Additional errors of misplacement of stress: _____

G

Emphasized words (focus)

Many words could be emphasized, but these should not be missed. If a word that gives old information is emphasized, this is an error.

[1] help

[2] Chicago, return

[5] cheaper

[7] prefer

[8] morning, evening, meal

[9] breakfast, movie

[10] which
[11] both, communities
[12] major
[14] west
[16] fare
[18] expected

H

Question intonation

[1] Can I help you? ⤴

[3] Of October? ⤴

[4] How much is the fare? ⤵

[7] What time ...? ⤵   ... morning ⤴   or afternoon ⤵

[8] Is there a meal ...? ⤴

[10] Which movie? ⤵

[16] ... what's the fare? ⤵

Quiz answer key

Master copies of the quizzes, which can be torn out and photocopied for students, appear on pages 79–86 of this Teacher's Resource Book.

Quiz 1

Unit 1: syllable number

Teacher: Read the directions out loud.

A Listen to the following words read twice. Mark the number of syllables for each word. (Count 10 points for each correct number.)

Examples bus   *1*
           busses   *2*

1. decided   *3*
2. planned   *1*
3. corrected   *3*
4. pleased   *1*
5. washed   *1*

B Listen to these sentences read twice, and write "past" or "present." (Count 10 points for each correct answer.)

Teacher: Read the sentences in brackets aloud.

Example You hear: We wanted to go.
           You write: *past*

1. [We plan all the parties.] present
2. [We planned everything for her.] past
3. [I need all the money.] present
4. [I painted my house red.] past
5. [We want some new books.] present

Quiz 2

Units 2, 3, and 4: stops and continuants

You will hear sentence (a) or (b) read twice. Circle the letter of the sentence you hear. (Count 10 points for each correct answer.)

Teacher: Read aloud the sentence with the circled letter.

1. (a.) Where is the bath?
    b. Where is the bat?
2. (a.) What is a tire?
    b. What is a tide?
3. (a.) They miss everything.
    (b.) They missed everything.
4.   a. We wash our own dishes.
    b. We washed our own dishes.
5. (a.) Please spell "curb."
    (b.) Please spell "curve."
6.   a. Have all the people left?
    (b.) Had all the people left?
7.   a. Do you know the date?
    b. Do you know the day?
8. (a.) How do you spell "rule"?
    b. How do you spell "rude"?
9. (a.) They'll answer everything.
    b. They'd answer everything.
10. (a.) Where'll Ann go?
    b. Where'd Ann go?

Quiz 3

Units 5, 6, and 7: voicing

You will hear sentence (a) or (b) read twice. Circle the letter of the sentence you hear. (Count 10 points for each correct answer.)

Teacher: Read aloud the sentence with the circled letter.

1.   a. Did you say "rise"?
    (b.) Did you say "rice"?
2.   a. How do you spell "leaf"?
    (b.) How do you spell "leave"?
3.   a. What does "have" mean?
    (b.) What does "half" mean?

4. (a.) What beautiful eyes!
   b. What beautiful ice!
5. (a.) What are the prizes?
   b. What are the prices?
6. (a.) Was it a big bed?
   b. Was it a big bet?
7. a. This seat is not right.
   (b.) This seed is not right.
8. (a.) Where is my cap?
   b. Where is my cab?
9. (a.) How do you spell "bug"?
   b. How do you spell "buck"?
10. a. Where is Gray's Alley?
    (b.) Where is Grace Alley?

Quiz 4

Units 8 and 9: stress

Listen to the following words read twice. Underline the stressed syllable in each word. (Count 10 points for each correct answer.)

Teacher: Read the words aloud, stressing the underlined syllable in each word.

1. ar<u>range</u>
2. <u>aw</u>ful
3. <u>ser</u>vice
4. <u>prob</u>lem
5. thir<u>teen</u>
6. eigh<u>teen</u>
7. Ne<u>bras</u>ka
8. <u>Can</u>ada
9. re<u>verse</u>
10. al<u>low</u>ance

Quiz 5

Unit 10: stress patterns

Listen to the following words read twice. Underline the syllable with the main stress. (Count 10 points for each correct answer.)

Teacher: Read the words aloud, stressing the underlined syllable in each word.

1. <u>cal</u>culator
2. infor<u>ma</u>tion
3. adminis<u>tra</u>tion
4. <u>phys</u>ical
5. e<u>con</u>omy
6. eco<u>nom</u>ical
7. <u>com</u>edy
8. com<u>mit</u>tee
9. <u>in</u>teresting
10. ele<u>men</u>tary

Quiz 6

Units 11 and 12: Basic Emphasis Pattern

Read the following sentences. Circle the content words. There are five in each sentence. (Count 2 points for each correctly underlined word.)

Teacher: The content words are underlined.

1. <u>What</u> <u>kind</u> of <u>books</u> do you <u>like</u> to <u>read</u>?
2. I <u>prefer</u> <u>biographies</u> and <u>serious</u> <u>books</u> on <u>history</u>.
3. <u>Where</u> do you <u>plan</u> to <u>go</u> for <u>summer</u> <u>vacation</u>?
4. We are <u>going</u> to the <u>state</u> of <u>Washington</u> to <u>visit</u> <u>friends</u>.
5. <u>What</u> is your <u>favorite</u> <u>food</u> for <u>breakfast</u> on <u>weekends</u>?
6. <u>Usually</u> I <u>have</u> <u>pancakes</u> and <u>coffee</u> with <u>milk</u>.
7. <u>When</u> are you <u>coming</u> to <u>visit</u> our <u>town</u> <u>again</u>?
8. We will <u>come</u> as <u>soon</u> as we <u>save</u> <u>enough</u> <u>money</u>.
9. <u>Who</u> was the <u>tall</u> <u>woman</u> I <u>saw</u> you <u>talking</u> with?
10. She <u>works</u> in my <u>office</u> and we <u>eat</u> <u>lunch</u> <u>together</u>.

Quiz 7

Units 13 and 14: focus words

Read these dialogues. Underline one focus word for each remark. (Count 5 points for each correct focus word.)

Teacher: The most likely focus words are underlined.

1. A: When is the next <u>bus</u>?
   B: <u>Which</u> bus?
   A: The bus to the <u>shopping</u> district.
   B: There are <u>two</u> shopping districts.
   A: Well, I want to go to the <u>best</u> one.
   B: Do you mean the best <u>quality</u>? Or do you mean the best <u>prices</u>?
   A: I want <u>both</u>.
   B: That's <u>impossible</u>. You would have to take <u>two</u> buses.

2. A: What do you do for <u>exercise</u>?
   B: Well, <u>nothing</u>, I guess.
   A: You <u>should</u>, you know.
   B: Yes, but I don't <u>like</u> it.
   A: Why <u>not</u>?
   B: Because it's <u>boring</u>.
   A: Not if you exercise by playing a <u>sport</u>.
   B: What <u>kind</u> of sport?
   A: Well, <u>tennis</u>, for example.
   B: Tennis is <u>work</u>!

Quiz 8

Unit 15: pitch direction of questions

Read these questions and then draw a pitch arrow (rising or falling) at the end of each question. (Count 10 for each correct answer.)

Examples When's the party? ↘
            When did you say? ↗

1. Where is the main post office? ↘	falling
2. Is it far from here? ↗	rising
3. Do I have to take the subway? ↗	rising
4. In which direction should I go? ↘	falling
5. Did you say "east"? ↗	rising
6. How long will it take? ↘	falling
7. Is it in a shopping district? ↗	rising
8. How much is a ticket? ↘	falling
9. I'm sorry. How much? ↗	rising
10. How can I thank you? ↘	falling

Glossary

The following terms appear in the Student's Book.

clear vowel   A clear vowel is said with its own sound. It is not reduced or made unclear (schwa). All stressed vowels are full and clear.
Ex. Africa

combination sound   A combination sound is made by combining a stop sound with a continuant (**T** + **SH** = **CH**, etc.). A combination sound is different from plain continuants.
Ex. **ch**eap/**sh**eep

consonant   Consonant sounds are made by bringing the tongue close enough to some part of the mouth to produce pressure.   *Exs.* sea**t**, see**s**

content word   Content words carry information and can cause a picture in the mind. (Compare *structure word*.)   *Exs.* cat, dance, smiling

continuant sound   A continuant sound can be continued as long as the speaker has air to continue it. (Compare *stop sound*.)   *Ex.* ba**th**

contraction   Structure words are often reduced (shortened).
Exs. I will . . . **I'll**
         can not . . . **can't**

contrast   The most important syllables in a word are made clear by different lengths.   *Ex.* Africa

   The most important words in a sentence are made clear by extra length for the stressed syllable and a change in pitch.

Ex. We're all waiting for you.

emphasis   Some words in the sentence are more important than others and must be emphasized to show a contrast with less important words.
Ex. This is my cat.

focus word   Focus words are the most important words in the sentence. They are emphasized mostly by pitch change to help the listener notice them.

Ex. We're all waiting for you.

full vowel   Full vowels are not reduced (shortened). All stressed vowels are full and clear. (Compare *reduced vowel*.)

intonation   Among other things, intonation is the use of pitch changes to help the listener notice focus words, different forms of questions, and the ends of thought groups.

Ex. What's new?

main stress   In a word with three or more syllables, there may be more than one full vowel, but only one syllable will have the strongest (longest) stress.   *Ex.* regis**tra**tion

pitch pattern   The musical change in the voice, up or down, which helps the listener to follow the meaning of the sentence.

Ex. Follow that car!   Which car?

question word   Question words are "what, where, when, why, how, who," etc.

reduced vowel   Most unstressed vowels are reduced (extra short) and made less clear (schwa) in order to make a contrast with the stressed vowel. (Compare *full vowel*.)   *Ex.* Africa

reduction   Words are made less noticeable when they are contracted or otherwise made less important. This reduction makes a contrast with more important words.   *Ex.* bread 'n' butter

rhythm   Rhythm is the pattern of long and short syllables.   *Ex.* absolute . . . have some fruit

schwa (ə)   Unstressed vowels are often reduced (shortened) and made less clear. This makes the stressed vowels more noticeable by contrast.

Exs. Africa, absolute

sibilant   A sibilant is a type of continuant sound made by placing part of the tongue so close to the top of the mouth or in a narrow valley shape (**S**)

so that noisy pressure results. This produces a hissing or buzzing sound.
Exs. **S**ue, **z**oo, **sh**ip, mea**s**ure, **ch**ip, **j**eep, bo**x**
(**S, Z, SH, ZH, CH, J, X**)

stop sound A stop sound is made by stopping the air flow so that it cannot be continued. (Compare *continuant sound.*) *Ex.* ba**t**

stress A stressed syllable is the most important part of the word and is mainly shown by lengthening its vowel. *Exs.* Africa, Alaska
— • • • — •

structure word Structure words do not cause a picture in the mind. They are usually not emphasized. (Compare *content words.*)
Exs. the, to, is, does

thought group A group of words that belong together in order to make sense. There is usually one focus word in each thought group.
Ex. "John," said the boss, "is crazy."

tooth ridge The tooth ridge is the bump which goes all the way around the mouth above the upper teeth. For **R**, the sides of the tongue touch the tooth ridge toward the back of the mouth, but air can still flow out the front. *Ex.* ba**r**

For **T** and **D**, the tongue presses the tooth ridge all around to stop the air flow. *Exs.* ba**t**, ba**d**

For **S** and **Z**, the tongue comes close to the tooth ridge in front to make a hissing or buzzing sound. *Exs.* bu**s**, bu**zz**

unvoiced sound Unvoiced sounds (**F, S, SH, CH, P, T, K**) are made without vibrating the vocal cords. (Compare *voiced sound.*) *Ex.* hal**f**

vibration Vibration is the rapid, regular motion of the vocal cords that produces voicing.
Exs. ha**v**e, see**d**, bu**zz**
(in contrast to hal**f**, sea**t**, bu**s**)

vocal cords The vocal cords are a structure in the throat that can vibrate to produce a voicing noise. The vibration can be felt by placing your hand on your throat while making a voiced sound. *Exs.* **v**an, **z**oo (in contrast to **f**an, **S**ue)

voiced sound Voiced sounds (**V, Z, ZH, J, L, R, M, N, NG, B, D, G**, and all vowels) are made with vibrating vocal cords. (Compare *unvoiced sound.*) *Ex.* ha**v**e

vowel A vowel sound is the most important sound in a syllable. It is made by holding the tongue far enough away from the rest of the mouth parts so that very little air pressure builds. (Compare *consonant.*) *Ex.* s**ee**

whisper Whispering speech is spoken so quietly that there is no sound from the vocal cords.

Bibliography

Abberton, E., A. Parker, and A. Fourcin (1978). "Speech improvements in deaf adults using laryngograph displays." *Speech and Hearing Work in Progress*, pp. 33–60. University College of London, Department of Phonetics and Linguistics, London.

Acton, William (1991). "Changing fossilized pronunciation." *Teaching English Pronunciation: A Book of Readings.* A. Brown (ed.), pp. 120–135. Routledge, London.

Allen, Virginia (1971). "Teaching intonation, from theory to practice." *TESOL Quarterly* 4 (March): 73–81.

Anderson–Hsieh, Janet (1990). "Teaching suprasegmentals to international teaching assistants using field-specific materials." *English for Specific Purposes,* Vol. 9, pp. 195–214, Pergamon Press, Tarrytown, N.Y.

Ballmer, Thomas (1980). "The role of pauses and suprasegmentals in a grammar." *Temporal Variables in Speech,* H. Dechert and M. Raupach (eds.), pp. 211–220.

Bolinger, Dwight (1989). *Intonation and Its Uses: Melody in Grammar and Discourse.* Stanford University Press, Stanford.

— (1986). *Intonation and Its Parts.* Stanford University Press, Stanford.

— (1981). *Two Kinds of Vowels, Two Kinds of Rhythm.* University of Indiana Linguistics Club, Bloomington, Ind.

— (1958). "Intonation and grammar." *Language Learning* 8: 31–117.

Bowen, J. Donald (1972). "Contextualizing pronunciation practice in the ESL classroom." *TESOL Quarterly* 6 (March): 83–94.

Brazil, David, M. Coulthard, and C. Johns (1980). *Discourse Intonation and Language Teaching.* Longman, London.

Brown, Adam (1992). *Making Sense of Singapore English.* Federal Publications, Singapore.

— (1991). *Pronunciation Models.* Singapore University Press, Singapore.

— (1991). *Teaching English Pronunciation: A Book of Readings.* Routledge, London.

Brown, Gillian (1978). "Understanding spoken language." *TESOL Quarterly* 12 (September): 271–284.

— (1977). *Listening to Spoken English.* Longman, London.

Catford, John C. (1987). "Phonetics and the teaching of prounciation." *Current Perspectives on Pronunciation.* Joan Morley, (ed.), TESOL: 83–100.

Chafe, Wallace (1970). *Meaning and the Structure of Language.* University of Chicago Press, Chicago.

Chela de Rodriguez, B. (1991). "Recognizing and producing English rhythmic patterns." *Teaching English Pronunciation: A Book of Readings.* A. Brown (ed.). Routledge, London.

Daneš, Frantisek (1960). "Sentence intonation from a functional point of view." *Word* 16: 34–54.

de Bot, Kees, and K. Mailfert (1982). "The teaching of intonation: fundamental research and classroom applications." *TESOL Quarterly* 16 (1): 71–77.

Fry, Dennis (1955). "Duration and intensity as physical correlates of linguistic stress." *Readings in Acoustic Phonetics.* I. Lehiste (ed.). MIT Press, Cambridge, Mass.

Fucci, D., M. Crary, J. Warren, and Z. Bond (1977). "Interaction between auditory and oral sensory feedback in speech regulation." *Perceptual and Motor Skills* 45: 123–129.

Gilbert, Judy (1992). "Demonstration aids for teaching rhythm and intonation." *Speak Out!* Newsletter of the IATEFL Phonology Special Interest Group, London, 10: 3–11.

— (1991). "Gadgets: non-verbal tools for teaching pronunciation." *Teaching English Pronunciation: A Book of Readings.* A. Brown (ed.), pp. 308–322. Routledge, London.

— (1987). "Pronunciation and listening comprehension." *Current Perspectives on Pronunciation: Practices Anchored in Theory.* J. Morley (ed.), TESOL: 29–40.

— (1980). "Prosodic development: some pilot studies. "Research in Second Language Acquisition. S. Krashen and R. Scarcella (eds.), pp. 110–117. Newbury House, Rowley, Mass.

Grosjean, François (1980). "Comparative studies of temporal variables in spoken and sign languages." *Temporal Variables in Speech.* H. Dechert and M. Raupach (eds.), pp. 307–312. Mouton, The Hague.

Gumperz, John, and Hannah Kaltman (1980). "Prosody, linguistic diffusion and conversational inference." *Berkeley Linguistic Society* 6: 44–65.

Huggins, A. W. F. (1979). "Some effects on intelligibility of inappropriate temporal relations within speech units." *Proceedings of the Ninth International Congress of Phonetic Sciences,* Vol. 12. University of Copenhagen, Institute of Phonetics, Copenhagen.

Kenworthy, Joanne (1987). *Teaching English Pronunciation.* Longman, London.

Leahy, R. (1980). "A practical approach for teaching ESL pronunciation based on distinctive feature analysis." *TESOL Quarterly* 14: 209–306.

Lehiste, Ilse (1977). "Isochrony reconsidered." *Journal of Phonetics* 5: 253–263.

Levelt, Willem J. (1989). *Speaking: From Intention to Articulation.* MIT Press, Cambridge, Mass.

McNerny, Maureen, and David Mendelsohn (1992). "Suprasegmentals in the pronunciation class: setting priorities." *Teaching American English Pronunciation.* P. Avery and S. Ehrlich (eds.), pp. 185–196. Oxford University Press, Oxford.

Mendelsohn, David (1993). *Learning to Listen: A Strategy-Based Approach for the Second Language Learner.* Dominie Press, San Diego.

Morley, Joan (1992). *Rapid Review of Vowel and Prosodic Contexts.* University of Michigan Press, Ann Arbor.

———(1991). "The pronunciation component in teaching English to speakers of other languages." *TESOL Quarterly* 25 (3): 481–520.

Nash, Rose (1971). "Phonemic and prosodic interference and their effects on intelligibility." *Proceedings of the Seventh International Congress of Phonetic Sciences*: 138–139.

Ohala, John, and Judy Gilbert (1981). "Listener's ability to identify languages by their prosody." *Studia Phonetica* 18: 123–132.

Peterson, G., and I. Lehiste (1967). "Duration of syllable nuclei in English." *Readings in Acoustic Phonetics.* I. Lehiste (ed.), MIT Press, Cambridge, Mass.

Prator, Clifford, and Betty Robinett (1985). *Manual of American English Pronunciation,* 4th ed. Holt, Rhinehart and Winston, New York.

Rogerson, Pamela, and Judy B. Gilbert (1990). *Speaking Clearly.* Cambridge University Press, Cambridge.

Wong, Rita (1987). *Teaching Pronunciation: Focus on English Rhythm and Intonation.* Copublished by the Center for Applied Linguistics and Prentice-Hall, Englewood Cliffs, N.J.

Clear Listening Test 📼

Name _____

Date _____

How you hear English is closely connected with how you speak English.

Part 1

Sounds   [10 points]

The following pairs of sentences are exactly the same except for one word. You will hear either sentence (a) or (b). Circle the letter of the sentence you hear.

Example a. Do you want everything?
     (b.) **Do you wash everything?**

1. a. They save old bottles.
   b. They saved old bottles.

2. a. She loves each child.
   b. She loved each child.

3. a. Was a bath all he wanted?
   b. Was a bat all he wanted?

4. a. He always spills everything.
   b. He always spilled everything.

5. a. Did she bring her card every day?
   b. Did she bring her car every day?

6. a. Which cuff do you like?
   b. Which cup do you like?

7. a. They've already gone.
   b. They'd already gone.

8. a. We can often see the mountains.
   b. We can't often see the mountains.

9. a. Who'll ask you?
   b. Who'd ask you?

10. a. We watch all of it.
    b. We wash all of it.

Part 2

Syllable number   [10 points]

How many syllables do you hear? Write the number.

Examples a. ease   _1_
        b. easy   _2_
        c. easily _3_

1. closet   _____
2. sport   _____
3. clothes   _____
4. simplify   _____
5. frightened   _____
6. opened   _____
7. first   _____
8. caused   _____
9. committee   _____
10. arrangement   _____

Part 3

Word stress   [10 points]

Draw a line under the syllable with the most stress (the strongest syllable). Mark only one syllable for each word.

Examples a. delay
          b. broken
          c. education

1. participating
2. photograph
3. photography
4. Canadian
5. geography
6. Europe
7. information
8. economy
9. economic
10. political

Part 4

Contractions, reductions   [20 points]

You will hear a sentence. It will be read twice. Write the missing words.

Example You hear: Do you think she's in her room?

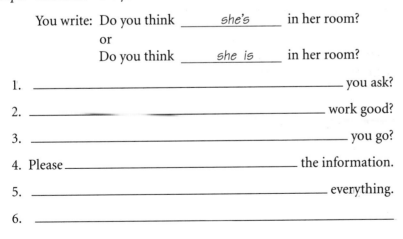

      You write: Do you think _____ *she's* _____ in her room?
              or
              Do you think _____ *she is* _____ in her room?

1. _____ you ask?

2. _____ work good?

3. _____ you go?

4. Please _____ the information.

5. _____ everything.

6. _____

7. _____

8. _____

9. _____

10. _____

Part 5

Focus: identification

[10 points]

You will hear a dialogue with ten sentences. In each sentence underline the word with the most emphasis (the strongest word).

Example A: That's a **great** idea!

A: Do you think food in this country is expensive?
B: Not really.
A: I think it's expensive.
B: That's because you eat in restaurants.
A: Where do you eat?
B: At home.
A: Can you cook?
B: Well, actually I can't cook. I just eat cheese.
A: That's awful!

Part 6

Focus: meaning

[20 points]

The following pairs of sentences are exactly the same, except a different word is stressed (stronger) in each sentence. You will hear sentence (a) or (b) twice. Circle the correct response.

Example a. They bought two bottles.   Not three?
     b. **They bought two bottles.**   (Not cans?)

Teacher: Give students time to read these sentences first.

1. a. We want to buy a lot of apples.   Not oranges?
    b. We want to buy a lot of apples.   How many?

2. a. I think that animal is a wolf.   No, it's a fox.
    b. I think that animal is a wolf.   Aren't you sure?

3. a. Frank wanted to go early.   When?
    b. Frank wanted to go early.   Who?

4. a. Sally writes the reports.   No, she reviews them.
    b. Sally writes the reports.   No, Bob does.

5. a. Does she speak French?   No, but he does.
    b. Does she speak French?   No, but she can read it.

Part 7

Thought groups   [20 points]

You will hear sentence (a) or (b) twice. Answer the question that follows the sentence you hear.

Example a. John said, "My father is here."
         b. **"John," said my father, "is here."**
         Question Who was speaking?   _____ *my father* _____

1. a. He sold his houseboat and car.
    b. He sold his house, boat, and car.
    Question How many things did he sell?   _____ _____

2. a. She likes pineapples.
    b. She likes pie and apples.
    Question How many things does she like?   _____

3. a. Would you like some soup or salad?
    b. Would you like some Super Salad?
    Question How many things were you offered?   _____

4. a. The president said, "That reporter is lying."
    b. "The president," said that reporter, "is lying."
    Question Who was speaking?   _____

5. a. Wooden matches are used to start fires.
    b. Wood and matches are used to start fires.
    Question How many kinds of things are used
              to start fires?   _____

Pronunciation Profile

Name _____

Date _____

This is a general list of areas which need improvement:

1. Stress and rhythm   <u>List</u>

    ___ Word stress (stress on the wrong syllable)
    ___ Sentence stress (emphasis on the wrong word)
    ___ Failure to link words
    ___ Addition of a syllable
    ___ Omission of a syllable
    ___ Failure to weaken unstressed vowels
    ___ Failure to lengthen stressed vowels

2. Intonation   <u>List</u>

    ___ Statements
    ___ Question word questions
    ___ Yes/no questions
    ___ Checking information with a question word
    ___ Questions with two alternatives

3. Sounds   <u>List</u>

    ___ Addition of a consonant or vowel
    ___ Omission of a consonant or vowel
    ___ Unclear pronunciation of a sound

Quiz 1

Unit 1: Syllable number

A Listen to the following words read twice. Mark the number of syllables for each word. (Count 10 points for each correct number)

Examples bus   <u> 1 </u>

           busses <u> 2 </u>

1. decided   _____

2. planned   _____

3. corrected   _____

4. pleased   _____

5. washed   _____

B Listen to these sentences read twice, and write "past" or "present." (Count 10 points for each correct answer)

Example You hear: We wanted to go.

        You write: *past*_____

1. _____

2. _____

3. _____

4. _____

5. _____

Quiz 2

Units 2, 3, and 4: stops and continuants

You will hear sentence (a) or (b) read twice. Circle the letter of the sentence you hear. (Count 10 points for each correct answer.)

1. a. Where is the bath?
   b. Where is the bat?

2. a. What is a tire?
   b. What is a tide?

3. a. They miss everything.
   b. They missed everything.

4. a. We wash our own dishes.
   b. We washed our own dishes.

5. a. Please spell "curb."
   b. Please spell "curve."

6. a. Have all the people left?
   b. Had all the people left?

7. a. Do you know the date?
   b. Do you know the day?

8. a. How do you spell "rule"?
   b. How do you spell "rude"?

9. a. They'll answer everything.
   b. They'd answer everything.

10. a. Where'll Ann go?
    b. Where'd Ann go?

Quiz 3

Units 5, 6, and 7: voicing

You will hear sentence (a) or (b) read twice. Circle the letter of the sentence you hear. (Count 10 points for each correct answer.)

1. a. Did you say "rise"?
   b. Did you say "rice"?

2. a. How do you spell "leaf"?
   b. How do you spell "leave"?

3. a. What does "have" mean?
   b. What does "half" mean?

4. a. What beautiful eyes!
   b. What beautiful ice!

5. a. What are the prizes?
   b. What are the prices?

6. a. Was it a big bed?
   b. Was it a big bet?

7. a. This seat is not right.
   b. This seed is not right.

8. a. Where is my cap?
   b. Where is my cab?

9. a. How do you spell "bug"?
   b. How do you spell "buck"?

10. a. Where is Gray's Alley?
    b. Where is Grace Alley?

Quiz 4

Units 8 and 9: stress

Listen to the following words read twice. Underline the stressed syllable
in each word. (Count 10 points for each correct answer.)

1. arrange

2. awful

3. service

4. problem

5. thirteen

6. eighteen

7. Nebraska

8. Canada

9. reverse

10. allowance

Quiz 5

Unit 10: stress patterns

Listen to the following words read twice. Underline the syllable with the main stress. (Count 10 points for each correct answer.)

1. calculator

2. information

3. administration

4. physical

5. economy

6. economical

7. comedy

8. committee

9. interesting

10. elementary

Name _____

Date _____

Quiz 6

Units 11 and 12: Basic Emphasis Pattern

Read the following sentences. Circle the content words. There are five in each sentence. (Count 2 points for each correctly underlined word.)

1. What kind of books do you like to read?
2. I prefer biographies and serious books on history.
3. Where do you plan to go for summer vacation?
4. We are going to the state of Washington to visit friends.
5. What is your favorite food for breakfast on weekends?
6. Usually I have pancakes and coffee with milk.
7. When are you coming to visit our town again?
8. We will come as soon as we save enough money.
9. Who was the tall woman I saw you talking with?
10. She works in my office and we eat lunch together.

Quiz 7

Units 13 and 14: focus words

Read these dialogues. Underline one focus word for each remark. (Count 5 points for each correct focus word.)

1. A: When is the next bus?
   B: Which bus?
   A: The bus to the shopping district.
   B: There are two shopping districts.
   A: Well, I want to go to the best one.
   B: Do you mean the best quality? Or do you mean the best prices?
   A: I want both.
   B: That's impossible. You would have to take two buses.

2. A: What do you do for exercise?
   B: Well, nothing, I guess.
   A: You should, you know.
   B: Yes, but I don't like it.
   A: Why not?
   B: Because it's boring.
   A: Not if you exercise by playing a sport.
   B: What kind of sport?
   A: Well, tennis, for example.
   B: Tennis is work!

Quiz 8

Unit 15: pitch direction of questions

Read these questions and then draw a pitch arrow (rising or falling) at the end of each question. (Count 10 for each correct answer.)

Examples When's the party?
　　　　　When did you say?

1. Where is the main post office?

2. Is it far from here?

3. Do I have to take the subway?

4. In which direction should I go?

5. Did you say "east"?

6. How long will it take?

7. Is it in a shopping district?

8. How much is a ticket?

9. I'm sorry. How much?

10. How can I thank you?